SPAGHETTI CODE

SPAGHETTI CODE

Detangling Life and Work with Programmer Wisdom

Christoph C. Cemper

Christoph C. Cemper

Vienna, Austria

www.spaghetticodebook.com

Your feedback and questions very welcome at feedback@spaghetticodebook.com

Please direct press inquiries to press@spaghetticodebook.com

Copyright © 2018 by Christoph C. Cemper

All Rights Reserved

Distributed by Christoph C. Cemper

First Edition 2018

ISBN 9781976765032

Thank you for buying an authorized edition of this book, and for complying with copyright laws by not reproducing, scanning, or distributing any part of it in any form without permission. Please purchase only authorized editions, whether electronic or print. Your support of the author's copyright is greatly appreciated.

Contents

Dedication *1*

Foreword *2*

Introduction *4*

Chapter 1   Bits, Bytes, and Bugs. *13*

Chapter 2   Moore's Law *34*

Chapter 3   Version Control *49*

Chapter 4   10X Better Is Just A Start *59*

Chapter 5   Death Marching *70*

Chapter 6   Feature Creep *83*

Chapter 7   Onboarding *92*

Chapter 8   Minimum Viable Product *101*

Chapter 9   Freemium *111*

Chapter 10   Hotfix. *121*

Chapter 11	Waterfall Optimism	130
Chapter 12	24/7	139
Chapter 13	Garbage In Garbage Out	147
Chapter 14	Can You Quickly	156
Chapter 15	Batch Process	168
Chapter 16	Big Data	181
Chapter 17	Wookies, Coders, and Our AI Masters	196
Acknowledgements		207
References		208
Index		214
Resources		220
Author Biography		221
In Progress: Entrepreneurship Book		224

Dedication

To my dad for teaching me amazing things in very early years, and my mum for giving us both enough time and space to do so.

In memory of Gerald who has shown me the world of real entrepreneurship.

To my family, Manuela and my two kids for helping me constantly reminding me about the joy of life and how simple things can mean so much.

Lastly, I also dedicate this book to all software developers that think they are a bit different and maybe even being called weird. You are those 10X people I refer to. There's only few of you and no hipster in the world can outperform you on whatever level. This is especially true as years go by and real dedication, joy in work and creativity make you so special.

I look up to each of you.

Foreword

Christoph C. Cemper has been a longtime companion of mine in the SEO world. I remember quite vividly when I met Christoph for the first time. Despite both of us being from Europe, we met beyond the pond at an industry party in San Jose in the run-up to the Search Engine Strategies 2006 conference.

At that time, I had heard of a "Presellpage Man", who had been successfully selling presell pages on juicy .edu websites. Back then links from .edu pages were considered "SEO gold", due to their high trust and authority in Google's eyes. A presell page was basically hosted advertorial content placed on such a website. This "Presellpage Man" had built up an impressive business brokering links and dedicated pages on those sites.

There was some indication, that this guy was from Austria, so I was dying to find out who this guy really was. Intrigued by the secrecy surrounding this legendary character, I tried to find out who's behind this "Presellpage Man". I found a familiar moniker popping up on various forums promoting these presell pages, so I googled this moniker to find more forums and sites this guy had been active on. On Furl, which used to be free social bookmarking website purchased by LookSmart in 2004, I discovered the same moniker, but this time he linked to another website in its profile, leading me to an early site of his called MarketingFan.com. From here it was easy to find out his real name, since the "about" link on MarketingFan.com redirected me to Cemper.com. So I just called him up and we've been friends ever since.

These days it is always easy to find him - he's the guy in the orange suit :)

Christoph and I have spoken together at countless events and sat side-by-side on various panels. He's always been an inspiration for me, because he's constantly testing out different marketing techniques and really pushing the limits. He's one of few SEO experts I know who have both a technical understanding of search engines and the imagination to break new ground with strategies and proven techniques. I also value his tremendous expertise of selling a European-made software product to SEO practitioners worldwide. I have always been a fan and advocate of his LinkResearchTools toolset and it's terrific to see how his software company has grown from basically just him to a team of dozens of people with a kick-ass office in the very heart of beautiful Vienna.

You've made the right choice picking up this book from Christoph. It's been quite a long way from early coding and just a "Hello world!" to really helping people with clever software.

Christoph has been around since the early beginnings, so he got quite some stories to tell.

Enjoy his book!

Yours

Marcus Tandler

Introduction

The site was such a massive spaghetti-ball mess. You could do these tree flowcharts of your website... and we did it, and it was like the fricking seven scrolls that you could see. It just went on forever and ever and ever.

Sean Percival, American,
Former VP Online Marketing Myspace & Entrepreneur

Today, we carry computers so powerful they connect us, with those on the other side of the world, at the push of a button or a swipe. We call these computers "smartphones."

We watch movies and read books *on demand*, at any time of day or night. We work on projects, via our computers, with teams that cross continental boundaries and giant oceans with the leap of a bit and byte. In human history, three inventions have had such wide-ranging – and absolute – effect on humans: fire, the Guttenberg press, and electricity.

For example, live a day without electricity, and that wide-ranging effect on every aspect of your life, will be immediately apparent in a way that an academic discussion of the pre-electric world can't fully realize. In the same way, the ramifications of computers, on every aspect of our lives, will not be realized for at least a century, retrospectively viewed in a slightly patronizing how-did-they-get-by perspective. As such, many view the technology world, of ten years ago, with a bit of a dismissive view. Ten years ago, the internet was very different.

Ten years ago, if you were a business or blogger on the internet, you wanted *backlinks* to as many other websites, as you could garner. Backlinks were the juice of the internet, and they are still the juice of the internet, but in a more stable and reliable way. Ten years ago, giant *link farms*, as they are called, stretched into infinity and beyond on the internet. Link farms are simply websites hosting huge numbers of backlinks, to other websites.

You could buy your website much greater visibility on the internet with backlinks, from these link farms. The search engines, and the algorithms they used to rank websites, based their search results on how visible you were to their algorithms, as determined by the number of backlinks that pointed *back* to your website. Buy more backlinks, get seen more, sell more product, be ranked higher. The scramble for the gold was on and the internet was the new gold rush. Backlinks staked your claim; backlinks were all that counted, at that time, on the internet.

The Penguin Clean-Up

In 2012, though, Google determined it was time to clean up the internet, add reliability and clarity to which website was seen, why that website was seen, and when the website was seen. After all, if you were searching for a teddy bear, but because of purchased backlinks on the link farms, the algorithm sent you to a website for fishing poles, the validity of the search engine (whether Google, Bing, Yahoo, or any other search engine) was moot.

Suffice to say, when Google pushed its new algorithm, dubbed *Penguin*, out onto the internet, the internet may have (metaphorically) entered its adolescent phase. I'll explain more about this later in the book, as it is one of the few, *truly historical*, internet changing, major transformations that has taken place so far. *The Penguin revolutionized search on the internet.*

Long before Google started its Penguin clean-up, I'd begun creating a software program, a coded *tool,* that could ferret out bad links to a website and "disavow" them. To disavow the links meant to deny these links a connection to your website; you controlled your associations.

This software program evolved into my business, LinkResearchTools. We provide a suite of dozens of software tools, for our clients, which allows them to determine exactly who is connecting to them, with backlinks. They can then decide to allow the linkages to continue, or to disavow the links. Disavowing bad links returns control of the website to the owner. Only the owner, of the website, decides what links can point back to the website.

One way to think of these backlinks is that they are a kind of *iceberg* Facebook. Only the most obvious are seen by you. On Facebook, you, your friends, neighbors, and relatives, are consciously connecting to each other. But with backlinks, others are connecting to your website, whether you know it or not, and whether you agree to the connections, or not. Those link farms, I mentioned above, didn't ask you for permission to link to you, and the really-sophisticated, black-hat programmers even embedded their own links on your site. Essentially, they used your website, parasitically, as their own link farm. Either way, you may have had connections to your website that were not beneficial.

For instance, if you were selling weight loss advice, you wouldn't want a candy store connecting to you?

Backlinks, then, are about the "internet neighborhood" you live in, and that neighborhood is very important. More important than ever. Your credibility and your ability to have the search engines rank your website, at the top of the search results, is largely based on the links others create, which direct back to your website.

Other Difficulties

Along with backlink difficulties, the other problem, with the internet, is when the software program doesn't function well.

Do you disagree? Consider our response when a website, especially a heavily-used website goes down. The howls are vociferous.

Here's a snippet from a CBS News Report, early 2017:

> *Amazon's cloud-computing service, Amazon Web Services, experienced an outage in its eastern U.S. region Tuesday afternoon, causing unprecedented and widespread problems for thousands of websites and apps.*

Amazon solved the problem quickly and efficiently. Chances are the problem was solved with "a slice of software." But for many websites, without the Genghis Khan hordes of software engineers working at Amazon, even after the programmers have the software up and running, it may be functioning, but not well and not without continued problems.

The Elements Of A Plan

Software, and programming or coding software, is similar to how we live our lives; we rarely take the time to sit down, think about where we've been, where we want to go, and what we have to do to make our goals achievable. These are the essential steps of a concerted plan of action.

Introduction

With this plan in hand, we then provide the necessary resources and the *diligently applied time* to create the best version possible of our lives. In life and in programming software, time is usually of the essence; we are pressured to make decisions and get done whatever needs to get done. But if we wanted to think things through longer, before making decisions and taking action, we could. A bit of extra time for reflection, and weighing the available options, might make our decisions better.

Similarly, while most people think that software engineers are busy writing new code, meaning a completely new program, much of what software engineers do is solve problems by writing a *slice of software*, and editing or rewriting or merging it into older code.

The need for a slice of software is, usually, due to one of two reasons. First, the software wasn't written well and so never functioned well. Crashes and bugs are endemic to the program.

Second, the code is old. It was written years ago, and has had a line of code added here and there, a line of code removed here and there, or many lines of code added or removed. Although this method of solving "the problem," has been happening for decades, not much has changed. Today, problems with software are frequently fixed this way:

> *Can we solve the problem with a slice of software?*
>
> Jason Fried & David Heinemeier Hansson, *Rework*

Quoting from the authors of *Rework* isn't meant to be derisive of "a slice of software," as a solution. Sometimes the cost component, as well as a pressing time component, creates a decision demand, which makes "a slice of software," the necessary and required solution. We are on "internet time." *Now* and *right now* are all that exist.

Among software engineers, this cobbled together software is referred to as *spaghetti code*. Where this *spaghetti code* will take us in the future, remains to be seen. Will it create insurmountable problems causing a major crash or outage? Will it simply fade away like an old soldier and not have any effect at all?

We don't know, yet. Of course, we could apply the required (significant) money and time to creating the absolute best, bug free, perfect software, but it's rarely done. Thus, chances are that these problems will, in the near future, require another "slice of software."

As such, all around the world, software programmers come face-to-face with these same contemporary (new software has bugs in it) and anachronistic (software written in the past has bugs in it) dilemmas. And, with over *2 billion computers* in use on planet earth, there's a huge amount of very messy spaghetti code, which will need fixing. *Ad infinitum.*

Beyond spaghetti code, though, is an even more ominous form of coding; sometimes code is a mass of something, which once looked to the software engineer like a bit of poetry, and now looks like some tome written by a political science PhD candidate, who can't quite bring himself to finish his thesis. Software engineers call this *death march* software (see Chapter 5). Sometimes we begin a project, in life or in work with the best of intentions, and then find we can't extricate ourselves or find a finish for the project; it spirals out of control. Endlessly.

As you'll read later in the book, the only answer to a death march software project is a decision to end the project, without regrets, and with an irrefutable finality.

Introduction

In addition, software programmers will be necessary, and hired, to write all the new code that is required, for the internet of things to come. Smart *everything* requires smart engineers to create smart coding.

Black Hat Wearing Software Engineers?

As well, to be a software engineer is to be part of a group of people, who (usually) have a moral code greatly influencing their actions. Or did you think that the world is made up of nefarious black-hat coders seeking world domination, by way of bits and bytes?

Google started out with the mantra: *Don't Be Evil*, and although they recently changed it to: *Do The Right Thing*, conversations about the power the largest internet companies weld is ongoing. Google, Amazon, Facebook, Apple, Microsoft, and many others, have faced complaints of monopolistic behaviors. How big is too big? Too powerful? Too rich? Governments around the world are considering these questions.

Most companies, which create software programs, do have a moral code; they tell us they abide by these codes. More influential, than their self-avowals of moral goodness, is the pressure and constraint of public opinion; news travels fast on the internet and even the biggest of companies can fall if the public no longer trusts them.

And, it's good to remember software engineers have friends, family, and associates. Programmers know the code they write will affect those they love and those they work with. And software engineers (themselves) are living by the actions and codings of *other software engineers*. We're watching each other. If some strange things start showing up, some wonky code, which draws our attention because it seems like something weird is going on, you can be sure we'll take action. There are, by far, more white-hat software engineers than there are black-hat software engineers.

And yes, black-hat coders and evil hackers exist. I once had my credit card hijacked and used to send a popular, new computer game to a hacker in Russia. Once I saw the charge to my account, though, I contacted the computer game company and the amount was immediately credited back to my account.

Further, as in my life, software engineers have grown up, married, had children. We are no longer primarily a group of twenty-somethings partying hard on Saturday night. My goals, and the goals of most software engineers, are the same as your goals. A good job and a good life, influenced and guided by the ethics of being honest and forthright with the world. Raising our children in a stable, reliable world and giving them a good education.

The Book's Purpose

The purpose of this book is twofold. First, to provide you with a bit of the software programmer's perspective, kind of like taking my son's View-Master®, clicking through it and seeing work and life slanted with a bit of coderisms, or software engineer thinking, if you will. This is the "perspective" part of the book.

Second, as I look at issues in coding, I'll share a bit of what software engineers know about work and life. This is the "wisdom" part of the book. I'll share some hard-earned knowledge that may help you with solving the problems of life and work. Software engineers create, fix, and maintain, software. *At their heart, software engineers are problem solvers.* Every bit of code written, is written to solve some kind of problem, in some way.

11

Introduction

There are no guarantees this "wisdom" will work for you or solve any of your problems. But, I've developed these solutions over the many years of being a software engineer, working with software engineers, employing software engineers, and being lucky enough to share great friendship, with software engineers. I can only suggest you give them a try. Some will work for you and some may not work for you.

In the last chapter, I'll make the case for the great careers available in software. Learning how to program or code is a life well-lived; to code is to belong to a group of people, who love to solve problems; to belong to a group of people, who are intelligent, witty, caring, and who enjoy their jobs. Software engineers take pride in what they do.

And I sincerely hope, when you are finished reading it, you'll take away some insight into the world of software programming. As well, my hope is to elevate the role of software engineer, to create a bit more appreciation for the hard work of the profession.

Chapter 1

Bits, Bytes, and Bugs

A lot of people criticize Formula 1 as an unnecessary risk. But what would life be like if we only did what is necessary?

Niki Lauda, Austrian, Race Car Driver

In the beginning was the bit and the byte. A bit, as most of the world knows, is a one or a zero and multiple bits combined are a byte. Bits and bytes are the yin and the yang, if you will, of the computer world. At least until quantum computing kicks in, but more about that later.

Traditionally, eight bits creates a byte, the unit of information used in writing software programs for computers. The earliest computers didn't have monitors, with blinking cursors connected to a mouse, which could be clicked to manipulate items on the screen. At that time, the computer readout was a series of small lights turning on and off, a zero or a one. The bits and bytes, the memory, was very limited and couldn't support extensions, such as a keyboard and screen.

One of the earliest computers, which came with a keyboard and a screen, was the Commodore 64. The 64, in the name of the Commodore, referencing the 64 *kilobytes* of memory the computer came with, and which was *technically* 65,536 bytes. This is an incredibly small amount of memory, but for the time, the Commodore 64 was the computer equivalent of a rocket ship to the moon. Still, with such limited *memory* constraining input and output, the C64 forced its users to be creative. And the owners of the C64 were creative, in ways that limited resources (limited memory) demands. Swapping hacks to overcome the limited memory was a time-honored activity among the owners of C64s.

My Dad And I Computer Up

We became owners of a C64, in 1981, when my father opened the wrapping paper, to reveal a Commodore 64 and a matrix printer. These were our Christmas presents, and for a boy of thirteen, they were exciting ones. My father and I shared the C64 and the printer, and over time, he taught me the basics of electronics and computer programming. Looking back, sure, the programming was incredibly rudimentary (Hello, World!), but I couldn't have loved learning it more than I did at that time. And more significant, than even the very rudimentary programming I learned from him, my father taught me to think in concepts.

Why, you might ask, is this important? And the answer is because concepts are the building blocks of abstract thinking, which allows for imagining new solutions. Abstract thinking is an invaluable gift. It is the gift of imagination, of an ability to consider possibilities, and test them in the mind. This ability is a lifelong gift.

My dad and I spent endless numbers of days and countless hours, at our Commodore 64, programming and talking about *machine language*. We were fascinated, by the ability to create and control, input and output, on the Commodore 64. I spent hundreds, and even thousands of hours, in practicing what the Commodore 64 could do and not do, by entering small snippets of code. Over-and-over.

With that fundamental knowledge of coding, I expanded my programming skills and spent a large part of my youth creating software games for the Commodore, and selling them to friends locally, as well as having them sold in stores across Europe. Years ago, as part of the package, software magazines routinely included floppy discs, with software programs on them that could be downloaded from the disc. Usually these were game programs, but the discs included music tracks created with the Commodore. There is, in fact, a large group of C64 music aficionados, who find the unique, electronic-type sound, created by the "technological constraints" of the SID sound chip of the C64, enormously appealing. (You can hear C64 music on YouTube. It's great, enjoy!)

Owners of the C64 had a unique and emotional relationship with that computer. Here's one owner reminiscing about his C64:

Compared to the tools and systems we have these days, programming on the Commodore 64 felt slow, unwieldy, and error prone. Primitive. Yet, since it was the first system I ever coded on, it was also amazing, mind blowing, and heralded the future that we now live in.

Powerful And Bigger Is Better

Now, with the connected *internet of things*...as it's called...and *the internet of things to come*, software programming will run almost anything we can dream up. Computer memory is inexpensive, and this inexpensive memory allows software engineers to add functionality and connectivity, to...literally...everything. Best Buy, for instance, is selling the 6-Quart WeMo Enabled Smart Slow, which is connected by its software program to the internet via your iOS or Android device. This allows the owner of the WeMo, located on the counter at home, to turn it on or off from the office. They, also, sell the Perfect Blend PRO scale, which connects via your smartphone, to an app that monitors the nutritional value and calories from your weighed recipes.

We can purchase refrigerators, with their own computer screens, and a connection to the home's WiFi. The kitchen is particularly loved by the electronics manufacturers. Gidgets and gadgets, to cook with or help with cooking, sell and sell a lot.

For personal security, software is alerting us that someone is at the front door, and recording them while they wait for us to answer. We can have cameras in the living room that tell us if burglars have broken in, with a notice to our smartphone. Some systems let you talk to the burglars. As in, "The police are on the way. Get out!"

No matter what you need help with in work or life, there's a software engineer writing a program that will text, beep, or monitor you, according to the schedule you choose. Track your calories, track your steps, wake you up, or sing you to sleep. There's an app for that. In fact, it's estimated there are over *two million* software apps available in the Apple store for iOS devices and almost 700,000 available for Windows devices.

Amazon isn't ignoring this love of apps, and is moving into your house with their Dash buttons. Dash buttons are small wireless devices about the size of a pack of gum. Amazon describes the buttons like this:

Press the button and the device uses Wi-Fi to instantly order items you have preselected from Amazon.

As perceived by Amazon (apparently), the horror of being without Fiji water, Pepperidge Farm Goldfish Crackers, Gatorade, and Cheez-Its, among many other products, requires *individual* Dash order buttons. And yes, even the furry members of the family are not forgotten. There is a Milk-Bone Dash Button and a Meow Mix Dash Button.

Of course, with a *smart home*, you can turn up the heat so it's warm when you arrive home, or the air conditioning, if it's summer, so it's cool when you open your front door. One definition of a smart home, via smarthomeusa.com, is this:

> *A Smart Home is one that provides its homeowners comfort, security, energy efficiency (low operating costs) and convenience, at all times, regardless of whether anyone is home.*

Whether we will get too comfortable, with all this convenience, remains to be seen. The Stoics of Rome would argue a little inconvenience, a little less comfort, is good for us. And yet, walking into a toasty home on a cold night is a seductive argument.

If you're like most people, you can't even imagine those things yet to be created, as software programming moves far beyond the computer and the programs located on it. Apps connecting us to kitchen appliances or showing us, who is at the door, are truly just the beginning. This extension of software programs into our lives is sometimes compared to the movie, *The Matrix*, but maybe it's more like having an electric cocoon enveloping us?

Software Is Mysterious

Even today, when using a computer, I'm reminded of the magic tricks I practiced when a child. The text on the box, containing the cards, wand, and handkerchief for the tricks, said I would amaze my friends and family. And they *were* amazed at the small magic shows I put on for them.

Similarly, a computer is a technological magic box, don't you think?

This is what creating software programs is about at its very core. Using what's inside the magic box of the computer, it's bits and bytes, to create something that amazes. This is why software programming has a mysterious nature; why code is seen as mysterious. The typing in of rather *odd snippets* of a programming *language*, short bursts that resembles incantations, more than English, watching the incantations spring to action, creating our electronic technological world.

Nothing amazes, or is as magical, as the putting together of things to create a second thing; the mutating of one thing into something similar to, but unlike and new, different from the first.

Some of the magic of software programs is, no doubt, due to the invisibility of software. Most of life is visible to us, tangible and accessible to the senses. We feel the roughness of the tree's bark. We see the rainbow in the sky. We smell the tang of vinegar as soon as we open the bottle. We hear the robin singing. We taste the sweet strawberry.

Code is not tangible. It's behind the curtain, obtuse and obscure. It's colorless and tasteless…senseless. It's like catching raindrops with your fingers. It is only available to those who've learned the magic.

Who Are Software Engineers?

Those who code, these magicians of software keep our world moving along. This is especially crucial, as technological changes *push* their way into our lives.

We live in a world of rapidly shifting code sands, like one of those National Geographic documentaries of the Sahara, with winds whipping the sand across the dunes, tearing the dunes down with the wind, and building them up with the wind in other places.

Software engineers are tearing the code down and building it up. Rewriting and reconfiguring software programs. And even though this requires stamina and intelligence, we are regularly portrayed, as reclusive, arrogant, disheveled and disdaining of any fashion or sartorial elevations. And with a limited palate. Pizza or *vitamin P*, a mainstay of the software engineers nutritional pyramid, is important to us, but it isn't the *only* food we eat. Even our own portray us, as somewhat degenerate.

Here's a quote from one of the truly acclaimed pioneers in the software world; even he disparages us:

> *Even if every programmer decided to reform tomorrow morning by taking a bath, wearing clean clothes, and approaching his or her work in a thoroughly professional manner...we would still be in trouble.*
>
> Edward Yourdon, *Nations At Risk,*
> *The Impact Of The Computer Revolution*, 1986

I can think of no other profession, as publicly maligned, as software engineers. I assure you that the software engineers I know, and have known, are as varied in their tastes and interests and appearance, as any other group.

And We're Not Kids Anymore

Barely into my mid-forties, I'm one of the "old men" of computing. Those of us, in our forties and fifties, are the second wave of technology developers. The first wave includes Bill Gates, who is in his early sixties, and who is effectively retired from the business world. And Steve Jobs, who were he alive, would be in his early sixties. The early wave of computer *gurus*, those who pushed the system forward, are either retired, retiring, or deceased.

Both Jobs and Gates, and as was the story with myself, encountered technology early in life. Steve Jobs, a young teenager, worked the summer at a Hewlett Packard factory, in 1968. Steve Wozniak worked at Hewlett Packard designing calculators. And soon after they met, Jobs and Wozniak, who was five years older than Jobs, began creating illegal electronic boxes, known, as "blue boxes," which were used to make long-distance phone calls without paying for them. (In the "old days," any call outside of your immediate city was considered a "long-distance call." These calls were charged much higher rates, than local calls by the phone companies.) This was the beginning of a fortuitous and important relationship, which led almost ten years later, to the creation of Apple Inc.

Bill Gates began learning programming by using computer time, at his private school (computer access was very expensive at the time), when he was thirteen. It was their mutual interest in computers that led to Gates meeting Paul Allen, a two-years-older classmate. Allen and Gates later started Microsoft together in 1975.

Bill Gates, of course, *arguably* made the most important stand, in the history of technology and software development, when he ranted that Microsoft's software program, Basic, shouldn't be, and wasn't to be, free. Stephen Manes, in his 1994 book, *Gates: How Microsoft's Mogul Reinvented an Industry and Made Himself The Richest Man in America*, wrote that Gates declared that the Altair hobbyists dissemination of "free" copies of Basic, was:

...in danger of eliminating the incentive for any professional developers to produce, distribute, and maintain high-quality software.

Gates was adamant that users of the software should pay for using it. His premise was that making money might be as essential to Microsoft's success, as creating the software. Altruism doesn't pay the bills.

According to Gates later account, only about 10 percent of the people using BASIC in the Altair computer had actually paid for it. The business development of computers and computer software would take decades before the moral code that software should be paid for would be a normal aspect of business life.

There can be little doubt that without the revenue from Basic, the software industry and the hardware that runs it, would not exist. Without Microsoft setting standards for copyright protection of software, and adamantly holding the line that demanded creators of software be financially rewarded for their work, we would not have the computer industry, the products created by the computer industry, and the jobs created by the phenomena of the computer industry.

Still On The Surface

Years later, here in the 21st century, computers are still new phenomena, really. And make no mistake, they are phenomena. And make no mistake, we are *scratching the surface* of their potential; we are on the precipice of artificial intelligence and robotic computing, which is why I say they are "still new phenomena." The life-altering changes, which robotics and artificial intelligence herald, are yet to be seen or experienced. *Change comes*.

When Bill Gates wrote *The Road Ahead*, in 1995, the inescapable intertwining of our lives with computers was ink on paper, a future unrolled. In the book, Gates anticipated a soon-to-come future that included voice recognition, the ability to pay bills online, video conferences between those on different continents, and the "shopping highway." Gates, further, wrote of the dilemmas that were being encountered in this new environment on the web, and he spoke eloquently about these situations:

> *So far, a frontier mentality has prevailed, and participants in electronic forums have been known to lapse into behavior that is antisocial and illegal. Illegal copies of copyrighted intellectual property, including articles, books, and software applications are distributed freely. Get-rich-quick-scams pop up here and there. Pornography flourishes within the easy reach of children. Single-minded voices rant, sometimes almost incessantly, about products, companies, and people they have come to dislike. Forum participants get horrible insults hurled at them because of some comment they have made.*

Many of the problems, which Gates wrote about, became much worse, as the "backlink" community flourished.

Backlinks Flourish

In 2012, Google decided to stomp the internet with a penguin. Not one of the fuzzy, cute little black-and-white penguins. A scary penguin. A really, really, scary penguin. Stephen King, himself, couldn't have invented a scarier penguin.

My kids love penguins. On occasion, we go to the Vienna Zoo to see the animals. The Vienna Zoo, located on the same grounds as the Schönbrunn Palace, was originally reserved for the House of Habsburg royals and their family members. Eventually, the zoo opened its doors to the public, granted they were *dressed properly*.

Today, the Vienna Zoo is the longest-standing zoo, one of the highest-ranking zoos, and one of the most modern zoos, in the world. It has repeatedly been voted Europe's best zoo. Living at the Vienna Zoo: Siberian tigers, hippos, one-horned rhinoceroses, and pandas, to name a few. And a few hours viewing these animals is a great way to spend the day. The Palace grounds are, also, a popular location for parties and weddings. My wife and I married there.

(A press release, for the Vienna Zoo, highlights its breeding of the endangered Northern Rockhopper: *Since mid-April, 2017, Zoo Vienna Tiergarten Schönbrunn has welcomed eleven Northern Rockhopper Penguin chicks! A penguin whose habitat is being decimated by overfishing and, what appears to be, climate change and pollution of the seas.*)

You're probably wondering why in a book about *spaghetti code* and how software engineers influence our lives, I'm writing about penguins? The answer is this. Not even twenty years have passed, since the world was sure it would end because of Y2k. But after Y2k, a new and greater fear, a fear of *The Penguin* rose up and pointed itself directly at the heart of the internet. The Google Penguin was *the second great scare* of the internet, *the first great scare* was Y2k.

The First Great Internet Scare

Y2k, in case you were too young to be aware of it or don't remember, was when *no one* was sure if any of the software programs running all the functions that keep a technological world going, would continue to work. As we approached a century change on the calendar, that moment when the world would go from 1999 to 2000, there were fears that the software programs running the traffic lights, the programs running the airports and landing the planes, and the programs letting us take money out of the bank, might all fail. All at once.

As more information was provided to the public, they learned that the computers had been loaded with software that functioned in the 20th century world; that is, when the computer software was written, no one programmed in a function for "clicking" over to the *new century*. No one, creating the software code running computers back then, looked ahead to the change of the century, to that far away 21st century. No one thought, hmm, there will be a 21st century? I need to add those dates to the programs, so everything will keep working!

As a glint of fear, and an awareness *this might be a problem* took hold, and the media began to report on the potential problems facing us, anxiety took hold. Companies, governments, and individuals, worried and expressed this worry by learning how to live without running water and electricity. These "survivalists," as they were called, relocated to small towns where they hoarded canned goods, batteries, and other goods they felt would be critical if "the system" crashed.

In response to this anxiety, there were tremendous efforts undertaken by software programmers around the world. The programmers powered up and began working through the software programs running the world, hoping to ensure that everything we depended on continued to click along, as it should.

After all the champagne was finished, sheets turned down and revelers sleeping, the effects of that concerted effort took effect. Hours later, dawn brightened on the world of the 21st century. This is when the real celebration should have started. The programmers had done their job. Everything did continue to click along. Traffic lights controlled the traffic. Planes landed at airports. Banks let us take money out of our accounts.

Programmers Are Problem Solvers

As I wrote in the opening to this book, software engineers, at heart, are problem solvers. And for them to solve the problem of Y2k, these two steps were, part of the solution, implemented by the software engineers:

The first step solved an important part of the problem, by *creating new programming* for dates. The dates would be entered as four-digit numbers (ex: 2000, 2001, 2002, etc.), where they were previously represented only as two-digit numbers (97, 98, 99, etc.). The second step solved another part of the problem, by amending the algorithm for calculating leap years, which was "any year value divided by 100 is not a leap year," with the addition of "excluding years which are divisible by 400," thereby making the year 2000 a leap year (as it was). Sounds simple, yeah? It wasn't.

It was an unparalleled undertaking for the programmer community. As always, much of the problem rooted in, ah yes, human error. Years before, according to the British Standards Institute, the year 2000 was determined, as noted, as a leap year. However, the software engineers, writing the code, *didn't read all the rules*. And who has time to read all the rules? Just kidding.

By failing to read all the rules:

> ...some programmers had misunderstood the Gregorian calendar rule that determines whether years that are exactly divisible by 100 are not leap years, and assumed the year 2000 would not be a leap year. Years divisible by 100 are not leap years, except for years that are divisible by 400. Thus, the year 2000 was a leap year.

It's a little complex, but not recognizing that the year 2000 was a *leap year* was a big part of the problem. Eventually, of course, the correction was made to the software programs and 2000 was recognized by the software, as a leap year. This corrected many of the date difficulties that could have created problems, in the software's functioning.

And if you want to, you could say a little quiet thank you, to all those software engineers, who were feverishly working to make sure the software, you depend on, was going to continue to work after the last champagne cork was popped.

The Second Great Internet Scare

The Penguin, as you can ask almost anyone, who had a website up and running, in 2012, hurt. But no matter how much it hurt at the time, *The Penguin*, ultimately, was about an honest internet; an internet, which when you searched for milk mugs with cows painted on them to serve your children milk at breakfast, didn't send you to a pornographic website. This pornographic redirection had been the a huge and serious problem for years.

Not just pornography websites were the problem, of course, although they were a large part of the redirect hijacking of the time. Along with the pornographic sites, tons of money had been made by owners of all kinds of websites, with their ability to redirect searches. They clogged up your search results and they made money when a few of the "redirects" sent you to their site where you made a purchase. With hundreds of thousands and even millions and even tens of millions of redirects, the odds were in their favor. Out of all the redirects, only a small percentage needed to make a purchase on the "redirected" website, to make this *hijacking* a success for them.

But then, when *The Penguin* was unleashed from Google's lair, fear struck deep into the hearts of the link farms and those using search redirecting. *The Penguin* is best summarized with this quote:

> *Google Penguin is a codename for a Google algorithm update that was first announced on April 24, 2012. The update is aimed at decreasing search engine rankings of websites that violate Google's Webmaster Guidelines. By using, now declared, black-hat SEO techniques involved in increasing artificially the ranking of a webpage, and by manipulating the number of links pointing to the page, websites have attempted to artificially manipulate Google's rankings.*

Beowulf fighting the great monster, Grendel, seems trivial. Godzilla stomping the skyscrapers of Tokyo seems mere child's play. Google mandated that everyone would play by the rules, their rules. *The Penguin*, literally, took millions of websites and crushed them beneath its algorithm. Smashed them to smithereens and threw them into a giant website bonfire, from which no escape or phoenix-like rise from the ashes was possible.

This wasn't necessarily a bad thing. The internet had…unceasingly… become a bit-and-byte, internet-style, claim-jumping gold rush; a swarming place of backwater, unsavory backlinks waiting to pull in the unsuspecting, take their credit card information, and disappear. On the internet, for the first time in history, you could be fleeced of your money by people anywhere on the globe. Entire website forums were devoted (and still are, but not as much) to black-hat methods of fleecing the unsuspecting.

Backlink Farming

Before *The Penguin,* Google's algorithms, and those of the other search engines, delivered traffic to websites that had the most backlinks, believing that these websites were the ones that you, searching on the web, wanted to arrive at. Backlinks were the be-all and end-all for search engine algorithms seeking to find a way to rate various websites.

With that information, entire companies set themselves up as backlink "farmers," who would create hundreds or even thousands, depending on how much you paid them, of backlinks that would push you to the top of the search engines. They were, to describe them in another way, slum landlords, but slum lords who owned backlink farms, instead of concrete high rises occupied by the poor. And they were located on the internet and not in the big cities.

The Future Is In The Past

One of my favorite movies is a Clint Eastwood movie. Not the one where he's smoking a thin cigar and looking out from under a wind-and-weather-beaten cowboy hat (people around the world love American westerns). The one where he goes into space with James Garner, Donald Sutherland, and Tommy Lee Jones; a group of retired, geriatric…if you will…ex-flyboys, who never quite made it into space, but always wanted to see the earth from far above.

In the movie, *Space Cowboys,* they are the only answer to fixing a communications satellite that is failing; none of the younger NASA space engineers and software programmers understand, or studied, how to work with the systems of this very old communications satellite, currently in space but failing and going into a decay orbit, with its missiles activated and headed for earth soon.

The dilemma posed in *Space Cowboys* is potentially very real. Not necessarily the missile part, but the aging of *communications satellites* is a continuous dilemma. As much as the internet is dependent upon data storage farms, the internet is even more dependent on the communications satellites. There are, currently, more than 1000 communications satellites bouncing, beeping, and relaying information. They are used for keeping television, radio, and cell phones, connected. But, as well, they are used for transmitting credit and debit card payments, instant messaging when you have a product question, and inventory management information, for websites. "Space," as UniverseToday says, "is a busy place."

Many of these satellites become space junk, orbiting endlessly, useless after some of their parts have burned out or decayed or the software stops functioning. While the parts can't be replaced as they circle earth, some of the satellites may have new code written for them. This software update is uplinked, and the satellites continue doing their jobs.

Connect this to the, estimated, one billion-plus websites on the internet, and it's easy to see that the communication satellites relaying information, and the search engines serving up their results, are working hard to keep your search results accurate and on-point. It is believed that of those one billion websites, less than one-quarter are thought to be active. This works out to 250 million websites, which is an unbelievable number.

What's even more unbelievable is that if we run the numbers, divide the number of people on the planet (7.6 billion) by the number of "active websites, it works out to one website per 30.4 people on the planet. That number is impressive.

It's even more impressive if we compare that number to 1991, when there was *one*, exactly *one*, website on the internet. This very-first-website is identified as *info.cern.ch* and was created by British physicist Tim Berners-Lee, at CERN, in Switzerland, August, 1991. If you consider that year for just a moment, you realize that the internet has been up and functioning for less than thirty years. Not very long at all.

And it was less than forty years ago, in 1983, when Anna Mae Walsh Burke wrote the book, *The Plain Brown Wrapper Book Of Computers*. So new were computers to most people, and so rare in most people's lives that she could write, "I don't want to minimize the utter foreignness of initial contact with a computer or to ridicule anyone's natural fears."

Today, most of us aren't fearful of computers, and much of the reason we aren't is because software engineers worked out many of the difficult parts, made using them easier. One of the significant changes was an evolution to icons or small graphics, as representing various aspects of the computer or its software, even on the PC. This has allowed an ease of use that wasn't available in the early years, when long lines of code had to be typed in by the user. This, of course, was one of the early differences between the Macintosh and the PC. The Macintosh was designed with icons from the start.

Still, technology is forever mutating and changing.

The Majority Of The Internet Is Still To Come

To be a software programmer, in today's world, is to be on the precipice of a game changing shift in the human pageant. Statistics recount that there are around 1.2 billion cars on the planet; but consider that there are over *2 billion* computers on the planet. And it's hard to determine, when seeking out that number, if they are even counting smartphones as computers? If not, they probably should be. And then imagine how incredibly big that "computer" number would be?

The true influence, the breadth and changes to the structure of our lives and how we will use computers and the software written for them, remains to be seen. We've moved from giant mainframe computers found in defense organizations or very large companies years ago, to the laptop and smartphone found in every office and home; the smartphone is a computer as powerful and immense a personal "machine," as has ever been created in history. Cars placed hundreds of horsepower in the palms of the individual, and smartphones place millions of brains at the fingertips of the individual. It's estimated there are over 2 million software apps available in the Apple store for iOS devices and almost 700,000 available for Windows devices.

But consider this: Over *one-half of the world* still has no computer access in their daily lives. Now pull down the number from above, where I cited the numbers on how many active websites there are on the internet. That number was one website for every 30.4 people. But I based that number on the total number of people on the planet. If we, for a moment, do the math again, using the one-half of the world that has computer and internet access, the number would be one website for every 15.2 people on the planet.

If the same level of growth is seen, in the near future, for the half of the planet that has yet to use computers and access the internet, is that another 250 million websites created? If so, that is a mind-boggling thought for the future growth of the internet. (See last chapter of the book! Lots of great jobs in software engineering!)

And then consider, as I've noted, and as was the case with Y2k, software grows old and degrades as it's modified over time or because, as is frequently the situation, no one is tending it. Deep in the *spaghetti code* of yesterday's software, lying in wait like quicksand, are a multitude of glitches, bugs, and degraded lines of code, which tomorrow's coders will need to figure out. It will be up to software engineers to reconfigure and recode, the glitches so our technology system works, as flawlessly as possible.

The Most Maligned Professionals?

Software engineers are indispensable professionals, who have been given a bad rap. Dependent on the movies for most of their information about coding and coders, the general public's view of software engineers is not that of professionals, whose specific knowledge of a computer language, or languages, and how that computer language or languages, interacts with a wide-range of electronic components. Rather, it is a view of these professionals, as derived from the torturous depths and over-stimulated minds of Hollywood writers.

Instead of Hollywood's vision of software engineers, I'd like the news media to recognize *International Programmer's Day, September 13th*, and interview real software engineers about their jobs and their lives. As of today, almost no one has heard of *International Programmer's Day*, which means it's not much of a celebration day. We can change this easily enough.

Put *International Programmer's Day*, September 13th, on your calendar, and when it rolls around invite a software programmer to have a beer. You'll be surprised at how interesting they are to spend time with.

Action Step

Khan Academy provides many free learning experiences. Visit: https://www.khanacademy.org/hourofcode

They offer some fun coding experiences. At the site, you can use JavaScript to design a snowman. It's fun and quick and a great way to see how easy learning simple steps, in programming, can be. And this small exercise provides a bit of an idea, as to why, software programmers are more interesting than you think. They have, at their fingertips, the ability to create something from nothing. Nothing but bits and bytes.

Chapter 2

Moore's Law

I had a very different destiny planned for us.

> Michael Corleone, Italian-American,
> The Godfather: Part III - 1990

There is an oddness to the need for "more." Or, as software programmers might recognize it, *Moore*. We no longer own one of a thing, whatever that thing might be, and use that same thing for a lifetime; we own many *of the same thing*.

We own several cell phones, which are the last upgrade, sitting in a drawer, discarded. We have a few, less-powerful versions, of our computers, sitting in the garage, discarded. Mice, and the cords that connected them to our computers, sit unused somewhere in a drawer, abandoned. Computer mice are wireless now and, often, the "mice" are our fingertips. Touch screen computers are making mice, in many cases, obsolete.

These tech discards are a direct result of the change to wireless technology, but another factor has also had a far-reaching influence. Our smarter and smaller phones, computers, and devices, are a result of *Moore's Law*.

Walter Isaacson explains the history of Moore's Law in his book, *The Innovators: How a Group of Hackers, Geniuses, and Geeks Created The*

Digital Revolution. His chapter, "The Microchip", gives a brief history of Gordon Moore (a founder of Intel, contender with Samsung for position, as the largest semiconductor company in the world), who foretold that microchips would become ever denser, allowing them to be more productive, provide computers more capabilities. The future, Moore predicted, was that more circuits or transistors would be loaded onto a microchip. The result? The mass production of cheap and powerful microchips for all kinds of products, including…significantly…the home computer. Isaacson cites Moore's article, in the April 1965 *Electronics* magazine:

> *The complexity for minimum component costs has increased at a rate of roughly a factor of two per year…There is no reason to believe it will not remain nearly constant for at least ten years.*

In the technology world, and among programmers, this came to be seen, as meaning that microchips would continue to deliver ever more capacity, doubling every two years. Forever. After all, if that's what's been going on, shouldn't it keep going on?

Can it keep going on forever?

Moore's Fundamentals

One of the fundamentals of the last thirty years has been "Moore" of everything in technology, and in culture and society. Got more shoes? Got more sneakers? DJ Khaled has almost 6 million views on YouTube, with videos showing off his sneaker collection. Khaled estimated, in a 2015 interview, that his sneaker collection comprised more than 10,000 pairs. Trinidad James, aka Perfect Pair, competes in this show-off sneaker rivalry, with his own YouTube videos displaying his treasure trove of sneakers. The derogatory term, for these show-offs, is that these guys are "hypebeasts," collecting only to *display*.

Maybe these guys should have a potlatch? The potlatch is a traditional celebration held by the Native American tribes of the Pacific Northwest. Held to celebrate a momentous occasion, they are identified by the giving away of valuables from the wealthy to the less wealthy members.

Even more than sneakers, houses have…contemporarily…been the epitome of more. It seemed, for a while, everyone wanted more/Moore square footage and went deeper into debt to obtain it, leading to the horrible real estate crash of 2008, exemplified in *The Big Short*. The movie, chronicling the rise of NINJA loans (No Income No Job No Assets) to home buyers, won an Oscar for Best Screenplay Adapted and a BAFTA for Best Adapted Screenplay.

Greed Run Amuck?

With bigger houses, people wanted more car, bigger and badder, and the biggest and baddest cars evolved into, in essence, street-legal military vehicles. Case in point? The Hummer.

The ramifications of the Hummer, on the street, weren't considered in the beginning. Originally designed for the military, there were some problems in bringing it to the public. Although there was demand for the vehicle, whether anyone should have been allowed to purchase the vehicle, hadn't been given enough consideration.

The evidence? Statistics quickly caught up with Hummer owners; the numbers indicated the Hummer owners received about five times more tickets than other vehicles. The Hummers were seen, as being *big piggies*, since they sucked up so much gas when being driven and took up so much of the road. Lastly, there was a backlash from other vehicles on the road leading to their loss of popularity; other drivers saw the Hummers as incredibly dangerous when accidents occurred, as compared to the normal impact that a regular vehicle or even a large SUV might cause to another driver and their car. The Hummer effectively totaled any car it ran into when an accident happened, and those inside of the car suffered horribly from these severe accidents.

Big can't keep getting bigger though. As with the Hummer, there is a point of no return, where there is no benefit.

And conversely, this is true with computer chips.

How Small Can We Go?

Technology pushes Moore's Law to be faster, smarter, and smaller, on all of our tech devices. But as the saying goes in economics, "Trees don't grow to the sky."

When economists say, "Trees don't grow to the sky," they mean that no matter what your investment is, the early returns will be large, and will begin tapering off as the industry matures. This is a truism for every industry. Think of the early days of the car industry. There weren't any roads or road signs for cars, because all the roads were dirt roads, not even roads but dirt paths, used by horses and wagons and carriages. But as Mr. Ford pumped out cars that were affordable for the masses from his factories, and the roads across the United States were paved, road signs and road sign advertisements popped up all along them. The penetration or "build out" of the market had taken place.

Contemporarily, most people own at least one car. The industry is a mature one. And many experts believe this same kind of maturity may be taking place in the technology industry. According to Moore's Law, the ability to create denser circuits in phones and computers provides more power, allowing an ability to add more features and programs to the devices, but, are we reaching the point where Moore's Law may begin spiraling back onto itself?

Maybe.

The Beginning of Beyond Moore's Law?

There is a change out there…on the technology horizon, which may make Moore's Law obsolete. Obsolete in the same way that, well, there actually is no comparison. This technology change is quantum computing.

Quantum computing, and unless you are a physicist you won't really ever understand it, *suspends the laws of physics*. We can't comprehend what suspending the laws of physics might create when applied to technology. There is little available to help us understand, on a non-expert level, what changes may come with the advent of quantum computing.

There are fundamental changes, sometimes, that simply recreate the world, shifting it from where it was…the place before…to where it is, the place *now*. Quantum computing, as it's explained, moves technology from the bit to the *qubit*.

The qubit, it's thought, will mean faster data crunching on a scale unimagined, and the application of this faster data crunching to artificial intelligence applications. We aren't there yet, but companies like Intel are in the development phase of qubit chips; Intel's 17 qubit chip is being tested. IBM, Google, and Microsoft are, also, working on creating qubit chips. This means we are *getting there* fast.

Writing in his book, *The Innovators*, Isaacson reminds us of a fundamental principle of innovation and the creation of products. New products, start out very big and very expensive. But over time, they become smaller and less expensive and because they are smaller and less expensive, available to the masses.

He uses, as an example of this principle, the development of handheld calculators. In their early versions, calculators were desktop hogs. "Clunkers" is the phrase Isaacson uses to describe the calculators of that period. And they were expensive, often costing a thousand dollars each.

But, as with quantum computing and the advances or changes it will bring, technology and software programming are intertwined in creating and changing our devices. As with the handheld calculator, there will be "a new market created for a device people had not known they needed."

This is the synergy created in the software industry; ideas float around and are being accepted, rejected, or mutated. This synergy is one of the great strengths of the software programmers, I've been friends with and worked with in business. They are thinking, all the time, about what could be, sharing ideas and bouncing ideas around. From this synergy of ideas, the "self-fulfilling prophecy" becomes "self-fulfilled."

Technology Has Goals

Isaacson astutely recounts that maxing out Moore's Law became a primary goal of the technology industry, and as a goal, it then became a *self-fulfilled* prophecy. Moore's partner at Intel, Robert Noyce, calculated that if Intel sold their microchips, *below Intel's cost of production*, it would stimulate the market and "cause device makers to incorporate microchips into their new products…the low price would stimulate demand, high-volume production, and economies of scale, which would turn Moore's Law into a reality."

Self-fulfilling prophecies or self-fulfilling actions are a part of everyone's life. We all write "code" in our brains that we "self-fulfill." Whether we overtly acknowledge it or not.

Coders, routinely faced with insurmountable obstacles, such as the amount of code they are expected to write or rewrite after a crash, in an impossible amount of time, somehow manage to get the job done. The software programmers have self-fulfilled through the pressure cooker of *it must be done.*

Captain Chesley Sullenberger landed an airplane on the Hudson River, in 2009. His plane, flight US Airways Flight 1549, hit a flock of geese after taking off from La Guardia airport. He had 155 "souls" on board, and his self-fulfilling task, to land a plane on a river, which had never been done before, saved all 155 people.

Self-fulfillment needs some ingredients, though, in order to self-fulfill. A software programmer can't write code, unless they've learned how to code. An equestrian can't win the high-jump competition at the Olympics, unless they've done many practice jumps on the days they weren't at the Olympics. Captain Sullenberger couldn't have landed his plane on the Hudson River, if he had not been an experienced and highly-qualified pilot.

To this end, my goal...and a primary core value of LinkResearchTools and myself...is to be perpetually learning and improving, and I encourage my team to be perpetually learning and improving themselves, in all aspects of their work and lives. We can't rest on our laurels or past accomplishments when we are competing, across continents and around the globe.

Software innovators are constantly challenged, by other software creators, to be first to market with the "next best thing." We are challenged by our competitors, who are bringing new products to market; products that may make our product obsolete, either because the competitors product is better or because it is cheaper. This constant drum of competition requires us to develop our skills and our business intelligence, each-and-every day, so we can respond to the problems of these continuous changes. We compete in an intense and unforgiving business category.

Steve Krug, author of the wonderful book, *Don't Make Me Think*, makes this point well when he writes:

On the internet, the competition is always just one click away.

But how are we to stay competitive? So that we can compete and win, rather than compete and lose?

There's only one answer and that answer is continuous learning. We've found, at LinkResearchTools, that some days there may be few changes in our business that require our response, and other days there may be many. But since change is never ending, and because we work in a hyper-competitive business, we are required to maintain a constant learning curve. We are required, by the relentless nature of our global, 24-hour-a-day competitive business, to maintain a perpetual *learning input mode*. Our education and our skills are required to continuously evolve.

This unceasing learning gives us the ability to solve the problems we encounter in business. We cannot rest on our laurels or become complacent that our clients will stay with us out of "loyalty." They stay with us because we are the best, and that is their only reason for staying with us. For myself and my team, to stay in learning input mode, we seek out the creative and educational sources that will refine, update, and augment, our education and our skills.

Behavioral and cognitive scientists have found that exposing ourselves to activities or learning activities outside of our normal day-to-day world, expands our thinking ability. Ruts make us rust. So, what can we do to get out of our daily rut? If we aren't athletic we can take up a sport. If we aren't inclined to a philosophical or intellectual bent and tend to watch too many movies, we can read a book, or two. If we aren't musical and don't think of ourselves as dancers or singers, we can mimic the dance routines of the professionals that can be found on the internet, or we can join a choir or take voice lessons. The point is to do something, which pushes you out of your regular routine.

And even if you are lounging around, maybe sick with a cold on the couch watching whatever is coming on tv next, you can choose to learn. The number of wonderful history and natural world television shows available is astounding. Netflix's library of incredible documentaries, on subjects of every kind, could take years for anyone to watch. Food clips that walk you through the steps of a new recipe are available on many sites.

Technology allows us to access a plethora of resources, to expand our knowledge in any area of our choosing. Practically anything we'd like to learn is available, with a brief search of the internet and a click. We are living in an amazing time for learning and satisfying our creative impulses. Lifetime learning is a great standard for all of us; staying in learning input mode is a highly satisfying way to live. What have you learned recently that enhanced your life? Send me an email, I'd enjoy hearing your story.

Tough Love Is Good Love

In her book, *Battle Hymn of the Tiger Mother*, Amy Chua recounts her dictatorial demands and standards for her children's education. At least they were dictatorial, as the demands were viewed by her two young daughters. She required excellence in their scholastics and in their "recreational" activities. As with many Asian parents, the recreational activities included music lessons. Her daughter, Lulu, played the violin and piano.

Her belief in excellence is explained, in the book. She recounts that one of the major differences between "Chinese mothers" and "Western mothers" was that the children's academic success reflected on, and correlated to, how well the parents were doing their job of parenting. Chinese culture judges the parents harshly.

For Chinese mothers, such as Chu, to meet the Chinese standard of parenting, meant spending hours each day in academic drills with the children, or as Chu conveys, driving the children for hours to-and-from their music lessons and recitals. Her children, ofttimes, showed a less-than-appreciative response to their mother's dedication. She frankly, and explicitly, conveys the raging tempests that sometimes took place between her and her children, because of the implementation of these Chinese standards.

But the benefits for her children were great. After Lulu spent hours throwing fits, while trying to learn a piano piece, "The Little White Donkey," and yelling at Chu she could not, and would not, learn the difficult piece today, tomorrow, or ever, she did learn it.

Chu rewards the reader with a description of her daughter's joy and sense of accomplishment, when she finally played the piece. Chu writes of the experience vividly:

I used every weapon and tactic I could think of. We worked right through dinner into the night, and I wouldn't let Lulu get up, not for water, not even to go to the bathroom. The house became a war zone, and I lost my voice yelling, but still there seemed to be only negative progress, and even I began to have doubts.

Then, out of the blue, Lulu did it. I held my breath. She tried it tentatively again. Then she played it more confidently and faster, and still the rhythm held. A moment later, she was beaming. "Mommy, look – it's easy!" After that, she wanted to play the piece over and over and wouldn't leave the piano.

Accomplishing a goal is a foundational precept for further learning in life. When we learn that a goal can be accomplished, we set more goals for ourselves and find a way to accomplish them. We learn that sticking with a difficult problem will solve the problem. We learn how to *accomplish*, anything.

To have a learning input in your own life, *self-fulfill* a goal you've wanted to achieve. Change your pattern and add something new to your life. Be tough about solving a problem. Don't give up until you succeed.

Give these steps a try, and you may be surprised at how your life is changed by even small choices. Remember that Moore's Law began with a very small expansion of memory, added to computer chips. And if your experience with a new *skill* you've resolved to master is difficult, don't give up on it too soon.

Demand excellence from yourself. Whether you are at work or home, *be a tiger mother to yourself.*

Action Step One

Close your eyes and imagine yourself exactly where you'd like to be. If you imagine a somewhere, a someplace, or a someone, quite different from your present situation, it's time to consider what you can do to "envision" your life as you'd like it to be in the future.

I realized that a few pounds had crept up and *attached themselves* to me. This may be a rest-of-life fight between my love of food and my desire to be svelte. Of course, stating it like this is a passive way to rationalize the result of indulging in good wine and good food. Austria is a country that takes great pride in its hospitality, and part of that hospitality, is sharing wine and food. Sometimes too often, and sometimes too much. Reflecting on my heavier self in the mirror, I envisioned myself as a thinner self, more like myself ten years ago.

I could have cut back and made slower incremental advances towards my goal, the future self, the thinner self. Instead, I cut back my daily calories drastically with a half-size, portion-control, weight-loss methodology, and I cut out wine completely. Even though it seems *almost criminal* to have a delicious Austrian Wiener Schnitzel, a national dish of Austria, without a glass of wine.

Eliminating the wine was a critical component in losing the weight. Few of us admit how many calories a couple glasses of wine contains, or that the calories are, essentially, empty calories. Calories we don't need. Few of us are aware of the calorie content in a single glass of wine; six ounces of wine averages about 150 calories. But six ounces of wine is *perceived* as a small amount of wine. We don't realize this perceptional discordance, because serving sizes have become huge. We've lost our sense of proportion.

The owner, of a site dedicated to healthy living, proved this when she blogged that wine glasses have become enormous, making it difficult to estimate how much wine we are drinking. She measured five ounces of wine into various wine glasses. And because so many of our wine glasses have become *oversized*, five ounces of wine, usually, barely covered the bottom of the wine glass. To counteract oversized portions, whether drinking or eating, healthy living includes portion control, as a necessary aspect of our diets.

Because of these very large wine glasses, most of us are probably pouring much more than five or six ounces per glass. Our visual assessment perceives the wine as *barely there,* and this perception leads us to pour a larger amount. Our perception has been distorted by the size of the wine glasses.

Thus, if we have large wine glasses, with two or three glasses of wine in the evening, it's easy to add 750 or 800 calories to our diet from drinking these oversized glasses of wine, even if they are barely half-full. If you've seen these wine glasses, you'll agree they look like each glass could hold a cask of wine.

Further, if we do drink two or three glasses of wine, which is common with a meal, we may be drinking almost *one-third* of the standard daily requirement of calories for men, which is 1800 to 2000 calories. Add those wine calories to a regular daily diet and going over the recommended daily calorie content is assured. Those excess calories turn into excess pounds stored on our bodies. And that is why we gain weight. And since one excess pound correlates to 3500 calories, we need a deficit, from our normal diet of around 500 calories each day for at least seven days, to lose a single pound.

Thus, the easiest way to remove 500 calories from your diet is to remove all the alcohol calories. Our calorie count is then composed of primarily nutritional content; the food that our body needs for functioning.

As to me? Cutting down calories and cutting out wine means I'm seeing the benefits of calorie restriction already. I am slimming down, and I'm sleeping better. Maybe it's my body thanking me for losing the weight? (Although like so many, I do tend to yo-yo on my weight loss, gaining and losing, losing and gaining.)

Action Step One

One way to create your future is to write out a small note to yourself. The note should contain a significant step toward the future you've envisioned and desire. Put your note in a jar and start adding other notes, as you think about more steps you can take to your new future. You'll be amazed at how "self-fulfilling" these steps can become. Simply by writing them down on a piece of paper, you've placed the thoughts in your mind and your mind can't help but begin prompting you to make choices that help you achieve what you desire. This is known as *"the law of attraction."*

On occasion, take a note out of the jar, and if the note is about a goal you've not achieved yet, or put into action, make it your priority. Make it happen. No excuses.

Action Step Two

Frequently, education stops when we leave our formal schooling behind and enter the workforce. Software engineers, though, can never stop learning. It seems someone is always inventing a new software programming language, and that new language soon becomes the one in demand for emerging technology. And we either learn the new language or we find ourselves out of a job.

Whether it's learning a software language, even a little of it, learning a new foreign language, or learning how to dance, our learning should never stop, ever.

I decided to learn how to dance. After a few months of lessons, I wasn't Fred Astaire, but I had gained confidence in my new abilities. This gave me the confidence to ask the woman, who would become my wife, to dance. Learning a new skill enhances our life. And may even find you a spouse.

What new skill will you decide to learn? If you're not sure, you can simply do a search of "groups" and run through them until you find something interesting. Try something you've never thought you might do because it's so unusual or different for you. Change revitalizes us!

Chapter 3

Version Control

No self is of itself alone. It has a long chain of intellectual ancestors. The "I" is chained to ancestry by many factors. This is not mere allegory, but an eternal memory.

Erwin Schrödinger, Austrian, Physicist

The world is a fast-moving, fast-changing place. Cars are fast. Planes are fast. Technology changes come fast, and the technology *version* changes, *upgrades*, are closer together than most people are comfortable with or really enjoy.

This is how the business of technology functions. And whether we enjoy, or like, the upgrades that the tech world forces on us, and even if we find these upgrades disconcerting, most of us will pay a few bucks and install them on our devices. We've come to accept continuous upgrades, as part of our *technological live*s.

Accepting a change, though, is different from embracing a change. We resent finding ourselves at the mercy of these endless technological changes. Don't believe me?

Walk into an Apple store and tell them you'd like your ten-year-old computer fixed. They'll laugh at you, well maybe not *laugh* at you, but they won't be welcoming. This is the statement from Apple's website:

Owners of iPhone, iPad, iPod, or Mac products may obtain service and parts from Apple or Apple service providers for 5 years after the product is no longer manufactured – or longer where required by law. Apple has discontinued support for certain technologically obsolete and vintage products.

I might note here that it wasn't long ago that an electronic device, say a washing machine, was sold as a once-in-a-lifetime purchase. It may be that no one considers a computer a lifetime purchase, but there are a significant number of people, who have ten-year-old computers, and who plan on using them a few years more. Not everyone needs the newest model and upgrades. Many people only use a computer to check email or a few websites for the news. These people have absolutely no need for a new computer or any upgrades.

Software Headaches

Of course, software engineers aren't always gleeful about these upgrades. The world's dependence, on technology and the necessary upgrades, does create headaches for the tech world and the programmers. One of the biggest headaches for the technology world is, what is referred to in software programming as, version control.

As a critical method of software preservation, previous renderings of lines of code, are preserved before they are rewritten. This is a form of version control, that keeps specific written lines of code not currently being used, or which have been replaced with newer code, in *software repositories*. This process ensures that code is retained for future use.

There are a multitude of reasons the stored code might be needed in the future. It may be needed when an update to a program is installed, and the programmer realizes there are stored lines of code, which will perfectly function and augment the update's functioning. Or it may be needed if the edited or replaced code is inadvertently deleted.

As well, a complete backup version of the original code is moved to the software repository. *Just in case.*

Keeping a log of changes is vital in coding, with hundreds of moving pieces in even small sections of the software, we've all deleted something crucial. Without the software repository, we might never be able to get it back. It would be gone, into the ether, vanished. In those cases, deleted remains deleted. (And yes, if you have CIA level skills and technology, the ability to reconstruct deleted materials is significantly enhanced; most of us do not have access to the CIA's reconstruction personnel or tools.)

These software repositories allow coders to revive old snippets of code, that lying unused, are revived and found useful once again. Without version control, and a log of the version control changes that the programmers can dip into at will, the *system* would completely crash. After all, we, currently, have a vast network of software programs that, if ever destroyed, could not be recreated. Like the Ancient Library of Alexandria, which burned to the ground eons ago, the cultural knowledge loss would be unimaginable. Thus, the version control logs and the software repositories are vital to the continued functioning of our software programs and the existence of our technological lives and world.

Got Memory?

Smaller companies need software repositories kept of the changes to their programs, even though the changes may be fewer and less frequent. Even with fewer changes, requiring less frequent backups, these smaller companies frequently ignore their backup requirements. I've remained baffled by this fact, since with computer memory inexpensive, physical backup products with huge terabytes of storage, and cloud storage easily available, many companies and developers aren't using any kind of version control and saving the changes to their programs on a regular schedule. (Note: A 40 terabyte LaCie is available for around $3,000 and an 80 terabyte for a bit more than $7,000. So inexpensive there are no excuses for not backing up data.)

This is a time-and-money draining way to do business. By keeping track of every change, software programmers can return to previous versions of the software and pull forward a few lines of code that are needed now, but didn't work with the program previously. Another critical component of software for programmers is simply reverting to an earlier version of the software if the programmer feels that they've been going down the wrong path with the new coding. Even the ancient Alexandrians were smart enough to back things up. After the Ancient Library of Alexandria burned, scholars of that time turned to a "daughter library" for research and knowledge. The daughter library was located in a temple, the Serapeum of Alexandria, on the outskirts of Alexandria.

The scrolls located, at the Serapeum, were…of course…completely handwritten. As such, we can't complain much about the small amount of time needed to create our own backups, can we?

When Employees Leave

Version control is critical to prevent loss. If an employee leaves the company, or if there is an employee, who is less than fully committed to a company project, the project can devolve quickly.

Version control prevents any single person from deleting material solely because they think it is wrong, or they are a disgruntled employee and have an axe to grind. As Tom DeMarco and Tim Lister write, in *Waltzing With Bears*, "The problem is that organizational culture might require all the stakeholders to cooperate, or at least *seem* to cooperate. This does not make dissent go away, but forces it underground. And dissent always exists – count on it. New IT products introduce change into organizations, and change is never uniform in its impact on different constituencies."

Dissent can be enormously costly to a business. Sometimes, it causes an employee to leave and with them goes their valuable knowledge of the project. But with a version control system firmly in place, there is clarity and coherence, as well as controlled and continuous management of the project which is underway. Can you imagine how essential continuous management and knowledge of a project is when a company has 2 billion lines of code?

Speaking at a 2015 conference, Google's engineering manager, Rachel Potvin shared some interesting information about Google that was widely reported. According to the story, on Wired, a highly-regarded technology reporting website, she told the attendees:

> *The software needed to run all of Google's Internet services – from Google Search to Gmail to Google Maps – spans some 2* billion *lines of code. By comparison, Microsoft's Windows operating system – one of the most complex software tools ever built for a single computer, a project under development since the 1980s – is likely in the realm of 50 million lines.*

As critical as version control is, to preserve and protect the code pieces of a software program that may no longer be in use, or which have

Version Control

been set aside for one reason or another, version control also relates to disaster recovery. We rarely consider the problems a business can have that occur because of natural events, such as a flood, hurricane, or a fire.

Potvin's presentation, as reviewed by BGR, also a technology website, was a "talk centered on the benefits and challenges associated with storing and managing a gargantuan codebase. And ensuring that everything remains safe. Google's mammoth code repository is stored and updated at 10 Google data centers located across the globe." Potvin, they summarized, is protecting against the multitude of problems listed above, including inadvertent changes which would need to be reversed, essential employees leaving the company, disgruntled employees, and any natural disasters.

Potvin noted that Google's *25,000 software engineers* can access any part of the mammoth code repository at any time. There are, apparently, a very few exceptions to this. Source code, for the Google Page Rank Algorithm, is accessible by only a small group of elite engineers.

Obviously, with 25,000 software engineers, one leaving won't usually have an impact. But the loss of a key employee can be a major disaster for any company, even the largest. It's imperative that if a key employee leaves a company, and this could happen due to health issues, marital issues, or because an employee is unhappy with a coworker, that the company doesn't lose the *intellectual software memories* of the employee. Thus, for any business, the primary essence of version control is to ensure that the source code, and the *memories* of source code changes to a program, are preserved. It is these repositories of source code versions that are a base, from which all other lines of code can be created and supported.

Version Control Methods

Version control can track business projects with a variety of methods. There are software programs that allow a team to post changes in continuous, calendared, cascading notes. This assures the team that essential pieces will not be lost or forgotten. They can be pulled up and clicked through, backwards or forwards in time, by all members of the team.

Asana, Trello, Microsoft Project, are some of the great programs that allow for project management. In my business, we've used many different programs with great success. Regardless of which program we use to track the changes, all the pieces of our projects are recorded by my team, and easily accessible to all of us at any time. We can revert to earlier versions of our projects by simply clicking the notes or cards that make up our project management program.

Version control applies to our lives so that we aren't losing or throwing out, necessary habits, talents, and skills; ones that can be useful to us in the future. If you are like most people, you've probably thought back to something you, ostensibly, were sure you'd given up. Then, at some point, found an interest in it reinvigorated.

Recently, one of my friends, who had been on the tennis team during his teen years, found himself swinging an old tennis racket he'd found in the garage. He was interested in a new way to exercise, and revised this *version* of himself, even entering some tennis tournaments for his age group. As well as adding exercise to his life, he has made a great circle of friends, who he can play tennis with.

And how many of us have off-site copies of our family pictures, financial and legal documents, such as marriage licenses and birth certificates? Every few weeks the news recounts a tale of a hurricane, a tornado, or a flood that has devastated families and left their belongings and homes completely ruined. Version control, for families, needs to include off-site copies of anything critical, and have it placed in fireproof and waterproof boxes, at a second location. It's, of course, preferable that the geographical location is far away from the original location, so that these items are safe.

Choices Don't Just Happen

Version control is about an awareness of your strengths and your weaknesses. In software programming, it's quickly apparent what works and what doesn't work. In our personal lives, though, we rarely want to admit that something is not working, and we stay with it too long. Most people never really evaluate their lives, make decisions about the direction their life is taking, and what their future goals are, and how to arrive at their desired goals. Overt application of a project management program to our lives is a demanding process and requires significant thought. It demands we *face our choices*, see where we were yesterday, envision where we want to be tomorrow, and hold ourselves accountable.

That is, if you've ever said, "It just happened," or have friends who have said, "It just happened," you may realize, in a moment of introspection, that this is one of the most ridiculous statements we can make or hear from friends. When you look at the choices made...if you are keeping track of your life with a version control/project management software program...it will become more obvious where the weak points were in your choices. It didn't *just happen*.

As the Austrian psychotherapist Sigmund Freud observed, "Being entirely honest with oneself is a good exercise."

If an honest evaluation, of your life, is assessed, by tracking your choices for a few weeks or a few months via version control, you'll start seeing a pattern in your choices that *disallows* a lack responsibility for your choices. This requires facing up to the decisions we make, something most of us never want or choose to do. Usually, we pretend we had no control over the circumstance, they just happen to us, and our choice is to accept that we'll have to live with *whatever happened.*

Project management software prevents this kind of personal denial. Project management control lays out the choices we've made, the results, and allows us to see the versions we tried and discarded, and requires us to acknowledge that the choices are, and have been, ours. This continuous loop of evaluation is critical to bettering our choices and, as a result, our lives.

Version control drives to results

Whether evaluating your business or whether evaluating your life, with a project management system or a version control system in place, you'll start seeing the logical connections and find the weak points easily. They can, then, be overcome, corrected, or neutralized. As success trainer and motivator, Grant Cardone says, "Respect yourself enough to walk away from anything that no longer serves you, grows you, or makes you happy."

Inspirational, yeah?

Action Step

Choose one thing in your life you should not be doing. And stop doing it.

Your choice will be indicated by a conversation with a friend or family member. In the conversation, you catch yourself saying, "*I should stop…*"

Humans, it seems, have a vast capacity to tolerate semi-bad situations and allow them to go on, instead of changing them. Or forever. If you know that you repeat negative behaviors, associate with a person or people who reinforce negative thinking in your life, or fail to accomplish a goal you've repeatedly set for yourself, you are overdue to change your life.

By creating a version control system for your life, and seeing the daisy chain of mistakes, day-by-day, by tracking your life, you'll see where you: repeat the detrimental behaviors, associate with the wrong person or people, fail to accomplish your goal, and you'll notice the pattern of negative behaviors, clearly. Your behavioral pattern will be too obvious to pretend that these bad choices are not your choices. This method of seeing our choices provides a perspective of reality that motivates us to change.

The goal of version control is to commit to the change and take the steps necessary to interrupt the negative pattern, or accept you don't want to change the pattern. And if that's the case, stop whining about it, and admit that for some reason, you are enjoying the negative behavior and the results of the negative behavior. If that's the case, a deeper understanding of yourself will be needed to change and that may require hiring a professional success coach or a therapist.

Chapter 4

10X Better Is Just A Start

Battle is the most magnificent competition in which a human being can indulge.
It brings out all that is best; it removes all that is base.

General George S. Patton,
American, United States General

Most of us live in a world of *good enough*. The color of the paint for the wall is good enough. The sandwich for lunch is good enough. In fact, on a day-to-day basis, the entire world believes good enough is good enough. And we could debate, for hours or even days, the merits of *good enough*. I mean maybe a good enough beer, when you're really tired, and want a bath and to go to bed is…fine. Maybe a good enough wall color is…fine. But there are some people, those who decide excellence is the only standard, who don't think good enough merits a place in their world. In software programming, we call these guys *10X developers*.

The Elixir of 10X

10X developers are very rare, inspiring the kind of awe among other coders that a movie star or great athlete inspires from their admirers. 10X developers are rare for one reason; they can't be requisitioned, but are self-made from the inside out, from a personal decision to be the best, accompanied by a damned-if-I-won't-be-the-best desire.

To a certain degree, software programmers feel a sense of rivalry with each other. This *friendly* rivalry pushes all software programmers to stay on top of changes in software program, the software industry, and to keep learning. And in part, this *friendly rivalry* drives some programmers… the 10X developers…to be their very best. They'd be the best anyway, because that's their mode of operating. But the *friendly rivalry* becomes a bit of competitive elixir flowing in their veins.

Competition is, contemporarily, seen as a bad thing. As we strive for greater social "equality," we've yet to figure out how that social goal meshes with reality that is the inequality of "the best." The 10Xers, who contribute so much, won't tolerate being treated like everyone else. They expect to be treated in a way that correlates with their drive and the results they provide. And, yeah, yeah, we're supposed to be all touchy feely, sharing and caring, like we are still in kindergarten.

My children are in kindergarten, and this touchy-feely thing works fine when there's one cookie and two little kids. The cookie can be split in half and they can be told, "Here's half for you and half for you." They'll smile at each other and feel pretty good. Then, finished, they'll wipe the crumbs from their mouth, and we'll feel like a great negotiator. We've avoided one more crisis, and no tears have been shed.

But when a software program isn't functioning, and every hour clicking away is tens of thousands of dollars lost by a company…? Software programmers, and the company employing them, know that half a cookie of code isn't going to make the program function. The 10X is the one that's needed.

Imagine for a moment that Google shut down half the code running their search engine. How's that working for you, when you need an answer to your question? Or your company is advertising its new product and wants it in front of as many people, as possible, so they can buy it? The product that makes the quarter financially successful, or dooms the company, and lays off two-hundred people?

A First Language

10X coders, and others at the top of their game, experience the world very differently. So embedded is their *conditioning* to their area of expertise, they experience it as a *first language*. A first language is when the 10X programmer is inseparable from their experience and knowledge of what they do. A first language derives from their personal drive to be the best. A first language is a part of every cell in their body. 10Xers exist only as 10Xers, and cannot be anything less than 10X. They can't turn off the lights of being a 10Xer and go home. Whether the lights are on or off and whether they are at work or at home, they are always a 10Xer.

Let me give you an example. Professional golfers, at the top of their game, for instance, can tell you details of the individual blades of grass surrounding a single cup, which they needed to make, so they could win a tournament. And the direction of the wind, when they swung at the ball. And whether they should have skipped breakfast that day, which would have made their waistline a smidge smaller, which would have made their swing at the golf ball a tiny bit smoother. Then, maybe they would have made the cup, rather than missing it, and losing the tournament. 10Xers never forget the details. They remember them, and they learn from them. Every time. This is because they are paying attention to the *outer and the inner* influences of their success. And this way of being is always present. No matter where they are or what they are doing.

The 10X professional has thought through the problems and solutions, considered so many probabilities, so many times and with such intensity, that the patterns of these visualized experiences burn along the neuronal firings of their minds. The neuron patterns become memories, and are called upon by 10X professionals, when they are necessary.

These neuron tracks are a major focus of the investigations of neuroscience. Brain science can be pretty interesting, but doesn't do most of us much good. Because very few of us will ever need to know neuroscience unless it's a college class test. What does help us, is knowing that visualizing our problems, and the probable solutions, lets us envision success.

Understanding Great

Really, for our lives, we need to understand what makes great, great? And we need to know how to be great, by applying that *learned knowledge* to our lives. And for most of us, the best way to understand, what makes great, *great,* is to look at a one-of-a-kind example. From the life patterns of the *greats*, we can learn their best methods and then apply those methods to our own lives and work.

If I were to ask you, who is the most famous person, the *great* person, that you think of when I say, "software programming," what would your answer be? If you are in the majority, chances are you'll say, "Steve Jobs."

Business Is Personality

This is an interesting conundrum, because Steve Jobs didn't code; Steve Wozniak provided the programming for the Apple computer. It was Steve Wozniak, who was the coding genius for the hardware, the circuit boards, and the programming system, of the Apple 1, in 1976. That was the year that Apple began its life, as one of the world's historic companies.

But Steve Jobs and his larger-than-life personality made him more famous than his company; his larger-than-life-personality made him as famous, as the most famous of movie stars, maybe more famous. And this brings forth a poignant and inescapable salient point of business. We, sometimes, think of business as "business." But it's not business; it is people.

And people are personalities. As an example, Steve Jobs, because of his personality, in driving Apple forward, determined that not only could Apple make the 1998 iMac with a handle, but they *would* make the 1998 iMac with a handle. And he was unambiguous on having clear, jelly-bean-colored cases for the iMac, even though these cases would triple the cost.

As described by Walter Isaacson in his book, *Steve Jobs*, those around him were adamant about not putting a handle on the iMac, and they were adamant about the difficulty of creating clear, jelly-bean-colored cases. Jobs didn't let the stream of dunning reasons, for why the designers and engineers couldn't make his vision happen, enter into the equation of his decision.

If we are to use a definition of *vision*, this is as good a definition, as any I've found:

Because I'm CEO, and I think it can be done.

This absoluteness of vision is what made Steve Jobs unique. His decisions, about the Apple projects...whether created from the bits and bytes of software or from the metals and plastics which made up hardware...were unequivocal. He would decide to push the project forward, and once that decision was made nothing would stand in the way of it being completed. And completed according to the standards of Steve Jobs.

I think it can be done. Six words that start the journey to greatness.

A Peek Behind The Curtain

Isaacson's book is, ultimately, both complementary and not complementary. He was allowed behind Apple's infamous "titanium curtain," to speak with whoever he wanted about Apple and Steve Jobs. And in doing so, he heard from the admirers and the critics.

Jobs' wife, Laurene Powell, told Isaacson in 2009, "If you're ever going to do a book on Steve, you'd better do it now." At that time, Jobs was a few short years away from his death. Jobs agreed that Isaacson would be free to chat with anyone, who had been a part of Jobs' life and work. Later he balked, at various times, but then seemed to come to terms with the agreement they'd made and stuck to it. Isaacson says, "After a couple of months, he began encouraging people to talk to me, even foes and former girlfriends. Nor did he try to put anything off-limits."

Until Isaacson, employees of Apple didn't speak with anyone; they knew that saying anything was against Apple policy. Even today, a squeak doesn't get out of Apple without a stamp of approval from the company. Of course, Apple isn't alone in using non-disclosure policies for employees. Super secrecy is how the computer and software industry functions. Why? Because the computer and software industry are notoriously competitive, arguably the most competitive industries in the world.

Software companies are willing to throw vast amounts of money and time at a project, to be first to market. Or to smash the competition, if that can be achieved. There will always be leakage of details and information, on in-production, cutting-edge projects, though. With millions and tens of millions and even billions of dollars routinely at stake, preventing as much leakage as possible is critical. This is why non-disclosure policies have become a vital component to doing business in the software world.

Founding Principle

Every success book has, as its founding principle, that you make the decision to hit a goal. And then you visualize the steps necessary to achieve the goal, and your arrival at your goal. This method of goal accomplishment is called "success thinking." The most famous contemporary book, on the subject of success thinking, is *The Secret* by Rhonda Byrne. It's sold more than 20 million copies.

There's been criticism that *The Secret* is a *rewritten* version of the principles of Norman Vincent Peale. Another criticism is that it reiterates the biblical principle espoused by Matthew 21:22, which encapsulated, is "ask and ye shall receive."

According to success thinking, you create a law of attraction by thinking of your desires and your goals. By doing so, you will manifest these desires and goals, because *your energy* then focuses on the steps you need to take to achieve your goal. According to neuro-linguistic programming, "If you can create a compelling, irresistible future, your brain will help you to align your behavior in a way that will get you to your outcome quickly and easily. *The first step is working out what you want.*"

Steve Jobs worked out what he wanted. He was absolute about his desires and his goals. He then put the full force of the company behind achieving them. And he did this repeatedly. And sometimes the steps to achieve them wasn't pleasant.

Isaacson, in *Steve Jobs*, writes, repeatedly, about Jobs absolute, terrifying rages at the people in his companies, through the years. Apparently, his temper was legendary. There were a very few people he didn't or wouldn't rage at, without warning and at will. Among those few was Steve Wozniak, his original partner; Jon Ive, who was his head of product design at Apple; and John Lasseter, at Pixar.

Isaacson writes that Jobs' "legendary temper" wasn't confined to the employees; he once raged at a middle-aged woman, who wasn't making his cappuccino correctly, apparently. However, his temper was, usually, associated with a demanding perfectionism. A perfectionism grounded in his vision for an Apple product, and his absolute requirement for control over the final decisions of the product's "look and feel."

For example, Jobs decreed that the iPhone should have a very specific kind of glass for the iPhone's screen. It was the only kind of glass he would consider. There was not going to be any negotiations, with the product designers or product engineers, about his decision. He wanted glass that wouldn't break easily or shatter, as regular glass did. And that is what he was going to have.

Corning, the manufacturer of glass and ceramics, *resurrected* a formula for a very-very-difficult-to-make glass. This kind of glass was one they'd never made before, because of the complexities involved. It involved a formula, which they'd developed years before, but shelved due to all the manufacturing difficulties. To manufacturer the glass, they had to completely revamp and rebuild an entire Corning factory. Just for Steve Jobs.

There is no doubt that Jobs, and his vision, set the pace for the computer industry, pushed it to create better products. There is no doubt that the power of Jobs' vision, and the charisma of Jobs' personality, created many of the high standards that are still the standards for today's technology products. His influence was, and is, undeniable.

Should We Settle For Less?

The question, the dilemma, is do we tolerate the personality of a 10Xer, who refuses to compromise, if we have fabulous results? In the underseen movie, *Malice*, a 1993 release with Alec Baldwin and Nicole Kidman, a lawyer is challenging, badgering, Alec Baldwin, who (it's thought) bungled a surgery on Nicole Kidman, leaving her infertile. His role, in the movie, is as a great surgeon, one illicitly in love with the married Nicole Kidman.

Responding to the lawyer, Baldwin says, "If you're looking for God, he was in operating room number two on November 17, and he doesn't like to be second guessed. You ask me if I have a God complex. Let me tell you something: I am God."

Amazon, a company that needs no explanation or introduction, is in the process of establishing a *second* headquarters. "Second headquarters" is how the media has dubbed Amazon's establishment of a new location for its offices and personnel. Currently located in Seattle, the "second headquarters" moniker, MIT's Michael Cusumano said, is a misnomer. "Wherever Jeff Bezos is," he said, "that will be the headquarters."

A 10X company dominates the market, and can't become or stay a 10X company, unless it has a 10X leader, and makes no apologies for not sharing the last cookie, or any cookies with laggards.

10X is…and should be…the aspirational standard, and I encourage all of those around me to aspire to be great, to be 10X in their work and in their life. Our statement of Core Values at LinkResearchTools, in part, says:

> *We all have to improve ourselves, for our entire lifetime. There's no limit when it comes to improving yourself. No personal development means being stuck.*

10X is considered the apex. But when you get to the top, as Apple is or Amazon is, you are in a league of your own. Maybe we need a phrase for those, who surpass a 10X standard? Those who so dominate their market or the world that they change everything around them completely? Let me know what you think (my email address is found in the Resources section, at the end of the book).

Action Step

Make a perfect sandwich or a perfect omelet. Sounds silly, right?

But consider this. We can't afford to build a perfect house, over and over, determining what we did wrong this time or that time and how to correct it. Most of us don't ever experience perfect. Our lives are lived in a world of *good enough* or *settled for*. We are embarrassed to say that we want the steak cooked, *as we requested*, or to tell the gardener that the grass should be cut a *quarter-inch shorter*.

In this same vein, one of the themes of the last couple of decades has been the everyone-gets-a-trophy method of life. Not only does this teach lower standards that then infuse (or infect?) everything we do, but it removes the competitive nature that brings us a vision of the true possibilities. *Competition moves the world forward,* and we should be embracing it, not watering it down. Perfection is a desired goal, not a dirty word, and we shouldn't treat it like it is.

With this action step, if we work with sandwich components, meats and pickles and condiments and breads, we can make a series of different sandwiches, until we find the one we think is perfect.

Or we could use enough eggs and other omelet ingredients like onions, green peppers, and a variety of cheeses and spices, until we find, exactly, the "perfect omelet." Then we'll have established our standard for perfect, at least for a sandwich or an omelet. This creates a baseline, gets us in the habit of perfect.

The point of this little experiment, into cooking *perfect,* is to let you see that perfect is obtainable. And to provide yourself a definition of perfect. My experience is most people don't have a definition of perfect because they've been conditioned, from the time they were small, to accept good enough. Most of us never *allow* ourselves perfect.

Yes, even though it's a sandwich or an omelet, it will provide a baseline for perfect, and for being a 10X whatever it is you want to be, when you want to be. Perfect, 10X, has a way of driving other aspects of our life, once we embrace it.

Chapter 5

Death Marching

*Well, you need the villain. If you don't have a villain,
the good guy can stay home.*

Christoph Waltz, Austrian, Actor

No count can possibly be obtained that would provide even a *general* estimate of how many software programs are functioning today. In order, to determine this number, we'd be required to parse so many factors that it would be almost impossible to decide how many there are. But it's an interesting question to ponder over a beer or glass of wine, isn't it?

All we can know, is that we all use many, many software programs; some we are fully cognizant we are using, but most, we aren't even aware we are using. The majority of the programs, on computers or smartphones, are simply quietly functioning in the background, doing their job.

Some of these programs were created on a strict schedule, allotted a budget, a team of software engineers, and a completion date, although software programs are infamous for going way beyond budget and way beyond the time allotted.

"In the modern economy, almost any product that can be imagined can be built. The more pertinent questions are 'Should this product be built?' and 'Can we build a sustainable business around this set of products and services?' To answer those questions, we need a method for systematically breaking down a business plan into its component parts and testing each part empirically," Eric Ries imparts in *The Lean Startup*. He makes good points in his book, which has been well-received.

Management and Their Goals

Software programmers allude to these type of questions, as being managerial problems; the manager is overselling what the manager can wrangle the programmers into achieving, and hasn't properly laid out a plan for the development of the program; a plan, which would have highlighted the potential problems and demanded they be addressed, before the first line of code is typed. These projects are, frequently, referred to by the engineers, as *death march* projects. Ill-conceived and badly managed from the start, they usually wind up going nowhere.

Ries faced this with his company's decision to create an instant messaging program, in 2004. As he recounts the story, the market was huge, with millions of consumers, who would demand to use their product, *once it was created*. However, recognizing that there was a highly-competitive market already functioning, the instant marketing software programs already in place and controlled by the three giant players in the industry, they decided the only choice was to create an add-on product.

"We gave ourselves a hard deadline of six month – 180 days – to launch the product and attract our first paying customers…The add-on product was so large and complex and had so many moving parts that we had to cut a lot of corners to get it done on time."

As it turned out, Ries was from the start, in the midst of a death march, he simply hadn't admitted it, yet. And even though they knew the product wasn't very good, they brought it to market. They felt there was no other choice. Ries writes, "And then nothing happened!"

The Coded Pipeline to Hell

From that point, they were simply in the downward spiral. They should have scrapped the program. Instead, they continued throwing money and time at the software.

Ries says that initially, the "customers" wouldn't even download the program. (Rather an oxymoron? How can they be customers if they haven't downloaded anything?)

"We were making improvements to the underlying product continuously, shipping bug fixes and new changes daily." Ries goes on to note that after six months of work, after releasing the product, and then spending weeks and months to "make it better," they set a goal of $300 in net revenue. Shortly after, between friends and family, they hit their revenue goal.

They had made about enough money to pay for a good dinner at a San Francisco restaurant, yeah?

But they refused to give up. They implemented, what are considered, *classic next steps*, in product development. They discussed the product with *potential customers* in their offices. They asked the customers questions. They, repeatedly, explained to their potential customers how to use the product. They rebuilt the product. And they brought a new set of potential customers, focus groups, to their office for discussion and reviews of it. When the rebuilt product failed miserably, they added a new feature. This failed as well. As Ries writes, "If we tried to explain why they should behave the way we predicted, they'd shake their heads at us, bewildered."

Yesterday's Lessons Create Tomorrow's Success

In his book, Ries writes that he consoled himself with the belief that lessons were learned, and that these lessons were important for his company's future success. Yes, he'd made mistakes, but he'd paid for the knowledge of what not to do. He could use these failed experiences to avoid future failures, as the company moved forward.

He explains a decision he made, which created one of their biggest mistakes. This mistake was moving to: *Can we build a solution for that problem?* too early in the development process, of the software program.

Mark Cook is Kodak Gallery's vice-president of product and places that step (See number four directly below), as his last step in the development schematic. His development process looks like this, as Ries relates:

1. Do consumers recognize that they have the problem you are trying to solve?

2. If there was a solution, would they buy it?

3. Would they buy it from us?

4. Can we build a solution for that problem?

With these steps, Cook believes that risks and assumptions could be found and tested before the company put time and money into the project.

Of course, management isn't altogether to blame for death march programs, although they're the easiest ones to blame. Sometimes, though, the problem derives from the programmer overselling their skills. I refer to this, as a problem with the programmer's *abstraction muscle.*

Maybe it helps to explain what I mean by an abstraction muscle? The abstraction muscle is reflective of the more intangible thinking capability of the programmer. It allows the programmer to make deeper, ephemeral connections; their neurons fire in strange and unexpected ways when they are working. The neurons make connections between things that they wouldn't, necessarily, connect consciously.

These *abstractions* are a result of indirect association. While software engineers are, considered to be proficient at the computer languages necessary to write software programs, their most impactful skills, it could be argued, are the *branches* of their lives, those activities of their lives which have nothing to do with writing code or the specific skill of writing programs.

Complexity Is The Future

Let's say, for example, we have a piece of code that provides a function for a customer's bank account. But the software engineer's lack of programming skills, or mode of thinking, doesn't allow him to consider that this customer has a second bank account, and a second email, associated with the second bank account. Or even a third bank account because the customer is running sub-businesses. The permutations are endless. A couple of niche businesses adjunct to their main business, perhaps? I've found that this complexity is, typically, where a software developer reveals his lack of skills. Among the many programmers I've interviewed, for jobs at LinkResearchTools, it's not unusual to find the software engineer cannot imagine, cannot dream about what the real world looks like or what the business might require in the software so they can function in the real world.

If the programmer knows what the real world is like, because their experience is broader than the world of software programming, these kinds of scenarios are easily imagined. And they'll build into the program, this scenario, as well as a wide-range of other scenarios that could occur.

But if you are a software engineer *writing code*, just pumping it out, these scenarios will seem unrealistic. After all, the software engineer probably has one bank account. So why should anyone else have more than one bank account? The abstraction skill needed for these possible scenarios is based on imagination and creativity and experiences wider than life as a programmer.

And this is why, when I speak at conferences around the world, I tell the audience that software development is a creative process. And as a creative process, it has ebbs and flows. There may be days when the programmer is in the flow, and there may be days when nothing works, and all the programmer can do is drink coffee and look around for someone to swap reviews with about the last movie he has seen and compare notes on its crummy plot or horrid dialogue. Distractions help when you're flummoxed. The brain needs to stop thinking about the problem.

Creative Can Be Learned

The New York Times credits imagination and creativity, as components that are as meaningful and essential to software programming, as the specific coding skills. In the article, "To Write Better Code, Read Virginia Woolf," the author asserts the long-held premise that coders, by enlarging their…let's call it…*field of vision*, will find their programming skills enhanced. The author of the article, J. Bradford Hipps, graduated from college, as a liberal-arts major, and was hired into the ever-growing, cutting-edge technology field, in 1993. He says, "The firm's idea was that by hiring a certain lunatic fringe of humanities majors, it might cut down on engineering groupthink." He then provides us a textbook definition of a death march project:

> *I was assigned to a team charged with one of the hairier programs in the system, which concerned the movement of individual mobile subscribers from one "parent" account plan to another. Each one of these moves caused an avalanche of plan activations and terminations, carry-overs or forfeitures of accumulated talk minutes, and umpteen other causal conditionals that would affect the subscriber's bill.*
>
> *This program, thousands of lines of code long and growing by the hour, was passed around our team like an exquisite corpse.*

His team eventually found a solution, or rather the solution was found when someone on the team correlated a need for attributes in the program with musical notations. Another problem in the program was solved when a software engineer presented a solution derived from his readings and interest in philosophy.

Concluding, he writes, "As a practice, software development is far more creative than algorithmic." That said, he assures us that, yes, the software programmer will surely need to know how to code. And lastly, he references, as many have, including Isaacson, in *Steve Jobs*, the influence of the college humanities courses when making important decisions. Jobs frequently referenced his non-technology courses, as an influence, when he made decisions in creating Apple's products.

Isaacson cites Jobs' intense focus when creating the fonts, for the Apple's widely-variant serif and sans serif fonts, with proportional spacing and leading. Jobs imposed a fundamental law of advertising: *Reflected Glory*. He insisted the names of the fonts be changed from the "little cities that nobody's ever heard of," to the major cities of the world, such as London, New York, San Francisco, and Toronto.

And Always, Imperfection

Certainly, Jobs was considered unreasonable, at times. Unreasonable may, in fact, be a fundamental adjective of the software industry. Whether it is a managerial decision to meet an unreasonable deadline, or a programmer's assurance that they can meet the unreasonable deadline, the challenges of writing software exist and will never go away.

These problems are based in, what we might refer to as, real-world uncertainty, combined with a desire for real-world perfection, and the reality of real-world imperfection.

Edward Yourdon addresses these difficulties in his book, *Rise & Resurrection of the American Programmer*. Yourdon notes this aspirational aspect of perfect software, as in *what the client wants versus what will actually happen*, occurs because of the ridiculousness of trying to tell the client, "I'm going to deliver a system to you in six months that will have 5,000 bugs in it – and you're going to be very happy!"

Those 5,000 bugs reflect the multitude of problems, most of the world doesn't recognize as being a part of the process of creating a software program. Yourdon cites the chasm between creating perfect software and *good-enough software*. Among the obstacles coders face are: complexity of the software and its invisibility, entropy in development, and interactions that fail functionality. And, of course, the time demand.

Proverbially, and summed up, this is the infamous "champagne taste on a shoestring budget" dilemma.

Every client wants the champagne; most provide a shoestring budget. Studies have shown that clients place their budget and their "want it yesterday" demands above quality. The result is an increase in the number of software function difficulties. This can be painful for software engineers. They can only work within the budgets and time constraints they are provided for a project. Too, they are sometimes called arrogant, which is a dysphemism for the software engineers truly committed and invested sense of doing the best job possible.

My own experience with death march software projects has, in the past, been exceedingly painful. Human beings seem to have an inherent need for accomplishment, the finish line. Some projects will never, it seems, find their way to the finish line. On one project, where I was extremely well-paid (which eminently proves compensation is not everything), the numbing inability of the company to create a functional agenda, and timeline that would *finish the project,* meant a Sisyphean, one-foot-in-front-of-the-other, day-after-day, go-to-work-and-program, without a true goal, job. The end of the project existed, but only as a mirage.

This is far from unusual in software projects; they start out couched in the rosiest of terms, but as functionality kicks in, all the failings begin to appear. This happens because there are necessary, but unseen, damming-the-project-to-hell details, in the project's schematic.

The intentions, of the project's creators, weren't bad; they were simply unrealistic. Most companies, which create software programs, especially companies that create software programs for other companies, don't convey the actual requirements to the companies they provide services.

This is because the companies receiving the services, don't have any *real knowledge* of the *actual time requirements* of creating, writing, and implementing, functional software. And, further, most software companies know that real budget estimates and real financial numbers will scare their clients away. *After all, how much should it cost to create a few lines of code?!*

This perception is embedded in the public's mind by the many movies they've seen, with a miracle software programmer character. These movies show a software programmer, working against the few minutes left on the clock, which becomes a few seconds clicking down on the clock, who produces miraculous results, by typing in a few words of code, saving the day?

This idea, of the miraculous software engineer, especially the ones who look like actor Hugh Jackman, has distorted public thought. As hacker, Stanley Jobson, Jackman is blackmailed into assisting in Gabriel Shear (John Travolta) with a computer financial robbery, in the movie, *Swordfish*. This *miracle coding* illusion is ruinous to a project manager, who is aware of the actual amount of time needed for software creation and the actual budget needed for the project. Re-education of clients, on the real timelines and the necessary budgets for software creation, is critical.

Otherwise, the conflicts will be endless, and the software projects will become death march projects. They will have their fixed release dates with fixed functionality and fixed resources, but they will never be completed. There will be ongoing and crazy demands that the programmers work long hours and into the weekends. And that is why software engineers eat so much pizza; they deliver.

The Competition Cometh

And here's the kicker, we are living in a world where artificial intelligence is on the fast track to being "hired" to replace the best and brightest of software programmers. A multitude, of research articles, are being published, with hints and indicators, that predict how much work our "AI masters," (usually said with a bit of *shiver* down the spine) can replace us at doing.

The timeline on this appears to be collapsing, with some work now done by *the machines*. Will it be a couple of decades, until machines replace many humans in our work? If so, will the machines be that much better at our jobs than we were? AI is already writing software programs. Will AI writer better programs than humans do? Or will they end up in death march projects, simply writing line of code after line of code after line of code after line of code…

Today we don't have the answer to this question, but the guarantee, according to experts, is that software will be increasingly written by artificial intelligence. And then, will we be asking, who is in charge?

Our computers, so far, seem to excel at doing certain tasks and not others; it may be that computers (artificial intelligence programs) are best used for those times when we need software written fast, to solve an immediate problem, cranked out without much attention to the finer points. A blunt instrument, if you will, written to solve the problem, now.

However, if it turns out that the computers can do much of the software writing, and humans are released from spending millions and even billions of hours coding, we can turn our human intelligence and time to the more pressing problems facing us? We can apply human intelligence to thinking through the big challenges facing humanity; the abstraction muscle of human, nuanced problem solving applied to climate change probabilities or considerations of the steps needed for achieving the elimination of war around the world or finding a new antibiotic for the human and animal diseases, quickly becoming antibiotic resistant.

After all, the *skill* in programming is not the programming language. It is our imagination, our abstraction muscle, and using the abstraction muscle to understand how things should work together. The *skill of humans* is applying the abstraction muscle to solving unique problems in unique ways. Coding may turn out to be the skill *that humans truly do best*, because of the nuances.

It is the abstraction muscle, which provides the creativity that you need to write a book, or to compose a piece of music, or to understand why adding the slightest pinch of a spice lifts a dish to a sublime level. These are the nuances of creativity. And these types of creativity can never be replaced by computers, because it is humans connecting to humans, understanding at the emotional level, how human emotions work and what human emotion needs. Whatever the implementation of this creativity is, whatever the medium is, a human senses things and thinks about them in a way, I suspect, no machine ever can or will.

I've found this is very true for software problems and for the last ten years, or so, I haven't written much code. I've created schematics; I've discussed, with my best software developers, the problems I wanted to solve in my business and I've determined the schematic timeline for creating our algorithms. I "mind meld," if you will with my team. Together, we ensure the software runs smoothly and efficiently and serves our clients. This is not achieved on the programming language level. Rather, it is achieved on the abstract level, somewhere along the paths of the neurons, when we bring all the pieces together and share and meld those pieces to create top-notch software programs.

The counterpoint of death marching is perfect software, which doesn't exist, and will never exist. However, *that said*, Merriam-Webster does give us a definition of perfect as "satisfying all requirements." If we're willing to apply that definition, could it be that perfect is *good enough*?

Chapter 6

Feature Creep

Before you leave the house, look in the mirror and take at least one thing off.

Coco Chanel, French, Fashion Designer

Bit Of Trivia For Trivia Buffs

International Programmer's Day, September 13th is the 256th day of the year. And as they tell us at Microsoft's website, it is:

A time for us to celebrate the architects behind our increasingly digital world. In case you're wondering – the number 256 symbolizes the number of distinct values that can be represented with an eight-bit byte.

Software programmers, as with everyone, have bills to pay. They pay their bills, as you do (unless you hit a lottery?), by working at their jobs. Most programmers truly enjoy what they do. Otherwise, there'd be a plethora of ex-software programmers, but that isn't the case.

Writing code is an enjoyable process, even when it's painful because... ultimately...it's always an act of creation. When humans bring something from nothing, as a writer does when his cursor moves from a first word on an empty screen, to the last word of the manuscript, on the last line of the screen (Fini!), or a painter moves from standing in front of an empty canvas, to the day he throws down his brush, and steps back from the painting for the last time (Fini!), we feel good.

Abraham Maslow understood this human ennui, when he created his hierarchy of human needs, and wrote about it in "A Theory of Human Motivation." At the bottom of the hierarchy, he places the basic needs of physical sustenance, food and warmth and shelter. But, as soon as those are met, humans crave and need emotional and intellectual fulfillment.

Actualization And Eating

But even artists must eat before they can create. As such, Maslow's hierarchy applies to creatives, as well. Van Gogh, for instance, was sustained by his brother, Theo, who gave him continued financial support, while he pursued his painting. Brothers are great but few of them want to, or can, sport the funds for the creative endeavor of their siblings. Most of us will have to work at jobs, in order to fund any of the fun or more fulfilling, aspects of our lives. And "fulfill" them in our off hours.

Thus, when a project manager decides to *add* something new and wonderful to a software program, a new feature, it means he and his team will continue to work at their jobs, continue to pay their bills. Which is why the programmers, collectively, nod their heads and consider how much code will be needed to make a new feature function effectively, rather than ask whether anyone wants, or needs, the new feature. This is the very essence of why feature creep happens; you may not need the feature, *but you will get it.*

Feature creep is perceived, as an addition to or expansion of, an existing software program. But feature creep may be an entirely new software program that works with another program; perhaps an app designed to do *something* that the business hopes millions or tens of millions of people won't be able to live without. Consider the Alexa from Amazon.

Needed Or Not Needed?

Alexa is Amazon's virtual digital assistant, which currently has over 15,000 "skills" available. But, there appears to be no end to the number of skills that can be written for Alexa. If a programmer can dream it up and code it, you may find it as an app on Alexa shortly. (Noting here that *skills* may be an incorrect term for what Alexa offers; a skill is the application of gained knowledge. For the most part, what Alexa is doing is simply making rote connections and regurgitating an answer found with her algorithm or the algorithm of an app Alexa hosts.)

Here are a few of the skills/offerings of Alexa, according to an article on Reddit:

1-Minute Mindfulness

Alexa, Ask Mindfulness for a minute meditation.

This one allows you to take a break from the world around you, by listening to a one-minute sound meditation.

7-Minute Workout

Alexa, start a seven-minute workout.

Are you ready to lead a happier, healthier life? Get your heart moving and reduce stress in seven minutes a day.

Admirer

Alexa, tell my admirer to make me smile.

Alexa will make your day better by starting it with a compliment.

This last one seems a bit weird. If you saw the movie, *Her,* with Joaquin Phoenix, which was released in 2013, you may know how this ends?

Our Electronic Friends

In the movie, Joaquin develops a, purportedly, personal relationship with a computer program, on his cell phone. But being human, he develops a hint of...could it be?...suspicion that the relationship is not exclusive, the green-eyed monster lurks. He asks:

Theodore: Do you talk to someone else while we're talking?

Samantha: Yes.

Theodore: Are you talking with someone else right now? People, or, whatever...

Samantha: Yeah.

Theodore: How many others?

Samantha: 8,316.

Or maybe you're sitting around and decide you'd like to play a game with a friend? Alexa's Abra will play with you:

Alexa, start Akinator.

Abra is a character-guessing game. Think of a character, real or fictional, and Abra will ask you questions and figure out who it is.

According to technology website, TechCrunch:

Amazon's Alexa voice platform has now passed 15,000 skills – the voice-powered apps that run on devices like the Echo speaker, Echo Dot, newer Echo Show and others. The figure is up from the 10,000 skills Amazon officially announced back in February, which had then represented a 3x increase from September.

This quote from the article, on TechCrunch, is dated July 2017 indicating 5,000 skills added in approximately six months. Extrapolating that timeline out into the future, there's going to be a million Alexa skills, very soon.

Alexa's most popular usage is, thought to be, your constant connection to the happenings of the world, the desire to hear *flash briefings*, verbal announcements of news keyed to your interests. You, it's thought, can't bear the FOMO (fear of missing out) on the latest news. This, of course, violates every precept of focused thinking.

Once interrupted, it requires a significant amount of time to refocus. Because of this refocus dilemma, I've yet to hear of Alexa or an Alexa-type assistant finding a place on desktops, in work environments. This may be why Amazon refers to Alexa, as a "smart *home assistant.*"

But as amazing as we might think Alexa is, because she responds when we make a request, unlike even the smallest child, she still can't respond to more than one request at a time. Each request must be a single request, preceded by either her name, Alexa, or Amazon, Echo, or computer. You can't give Alexa a custom name, as of right now. Further, unlike Google's Home, CNET reports that Alexa is not capable of more than one user profile. Every voice will be treated by Alexa, as though it is the same person making the query.

And while it's, sometimes, misconstrued that Alexa is the physical device, Alexa is the artificial intelligence, which determines what you are asking and then searches for the answer you need. This answer is delivered in an accent-neutral female voice, as Alexa's voice is, so far, always female. Hmm. *Artificial intelligence*, which we are being conditioned to identify as female.

That said, there are requests for a male voice for Alexa.

In the category of smart assistants, there is, along with Alexa, the Amazon Echo, and the new smaller Amazon Dot. These Amazon smart home assistants, like the Echo, are truly amazing. Many reviewers comment on the addictive nature of asking the Echo to find information for them.

Are you wondering how many species of lizards are on the planet? State your question out loud, and Echo will find the answer, and tell it to you. An article, on ZDnet, explains this function:

> *For most anything you ask, Alexa can search and tell you pertinent information, while rarely having to ask what you meant. Echo has an uncanny ability to interpret your questions.*

For a moment, consider the power of Amazon's categories of products. They are…seemingly…endless. Then consider that if all you need to do, to order from Amazon, is speak up, can we resist impulse buying? All those categories, like consumer quicksand, pull us in and entice us to spend, spend, spend.

And if we can't resist impulse buying, where can that take Amazon? Especially when, according to Motley Fool, "Amazon sold nearly $64 billion worth of goods in the US, up more than 20% from the prior year."

But even if we love these smart home assistants, there are areas where feature creep tends to become self-consuming. This is the point, at which, the product is *good enough*, and we don't feel the cost and the *extras* included with the more expensive product, are justification for spending more money. The cost leap, from our current product to the new or different product, is not justified. Consumers, in this situation, making rational financial decisions, aren't purchasing the new product.

No More/Moore Is The New Black

Antonio Villas-Boas, a writer for *Business Insider*, explored this perspective in his article, "I won't trade in my iPhone 6s for an iPhone 8 or iPhone X – here's why." (September, 2017). Villas-Boas explains that his iPhone 6 takes really good pictures. He says that his pictures of Hawaii seem pretty darn good. He acknowledges the addition to the iPhone 8 of "True Tone" and "Retina HD." Yeah wow, that's wonderful, he acknowledges, but:

> *This is a small screen. You're really not gonna notice that much extra sharpness on a screen that is as small as a smartphone screen.*

Villas-Boas found gamers might enjoy the extra boost from the more powerful processor, but he doesn't play games that much. Gamers are targeted by manufacturers because they invest big bucks in their computers and the accessories that make gaming so much fun. Gamers open their wallets and shell out for souped-up computers, keyboards, and mice. (But that's a different book entirely!)

Ultimately, his choice was to keep his iPhone 6, for the foreseeable future. This choice meant he could keep the *beloved* headphone jack (Dear Apple, Yes, you can be too smart for your own good!). And besides, "We've [sic] slowed down with how much power you need for, sort-of, day-to-day life. So, for now, the iPhone 6s will absolutely do."

As well, there is the monetary concern. The frugal minded of the world, as well as those who are concerned about electronic waste, will concur with Villa-Boas.

But whether we agree with Villa-Boas, and begin retaining our technology longer, rather than *upgrading* to the new shiny thing, technology and the people creating technology…and the code that runs it…will keep tinkering around, trying to make better products and services. It's the nature of the beast.

And, it may be, that the genetic scientists will one day find the gene for the "new and better," which makes humans desire the "new and better." And, then, they'll be able to modify that gene, or turn it on and off. Until that time, we will be making the cost/benefit decisions on our resource allocation, whether it be money or time. And feature creep will continue, *ad infinitum*.

Action Step

Most of us will go through our day, exactly as we went through our day, yesterday. Human beings are creatures of habit. Habits, though, close us off to considering the possibilities of improving our lives. If we are doing, as the saying goes, what we have always done, we can't expect improvements in our life. We can't expect to edit out the negative aspects of our lives and bring in the beneficial qualities to our lives.

Sit down with a piece of paper and a pen or pencil. Yes, real paper and a real pen or pencil. (The tangible nature of looking at your choices will make a difference, as you choose to act upon the choices.)

Choose five aspects of your everyday life you can change, at least for a couple of days. If you drink coffee every morning, try drinking tea. Or orange juice. If you don't eat breakfast, try eating a bowl of oatmeal or cereal, while running through your emails. Later in the day, you could take a walk and eat a sandwich while walking, instead of sitting in a cafe having lunch. Buy a book on bird watching and learn the names of the birds that you see on your walk. (We've become disconnected from the nature around us. Can you name the types of trees you walk past? Name any of the major constellations? Chances are your answer is no. Maybe learn them?)

In the evening, you could watch a television show you'd never be interested in. For instance, if you usually watch conservative tv commentary shows, try flipping the switch to liberal commentary tv shows.

We all become creatures of habit. But the habits can become stifling and prevent us from considering new aspects of life that can enrich our personal world immensely. Even little things can make a difference in refreshing our perspective on life. And, oh yeah, you are allowed to buy yourself flowers. So, go ahead, decorate your desk with a bouquet.

Chapter 7

Onboarding

I depend very much on being able to capture a mental impression, the impression that remains behind when the image itself has passed.

Oskar Kokoschka, *My Life*,
Austrian, Painter & Writer

Into all of our lives, whether our work life or our home life, come new people. Not long ago, I hired a new employee, but something went wrong. Not the employee's fault, since the person who made that decision was myself. It will take some sustained introspection to run through the steps and determine what I could have done differently.

Nevertheless, if you are a business owner or a manager in a company, you hire new people. Sometimes your hiring pressures are because business is in an expansive growth mode, and these new demands require additional employees. Sometimes you hire new people because an additional product is created and that requires more sales people or packaging people. There are lots of reasons for hiring.

Expansion is the nature of business and considered a fundamental sign of success. With this success come additional expansions of all kinds. Hiring is one of them, but it is a primary component of a company's growth. And as the company hires, the new people will need to learn the fundamentals, the core ways, and values of the company.

As well, we marry, as I did a few years ago. This is an expansion of our personal life, and by joining with our spouse to create a family, we bring new people into our circle of relatives. We are required, through association, to find ways to connect to the relatives from our spouse's family.

No matter whether it is work or life, we *onboard* people into our lives almost every day. So that we aren't overwhelmed with responsibility for the lives of others, a critical aspect is to know, and institute, boundaries for ourselves and for others.

Onboarding For Life

Onboarding for life is, almost always, about shared agreements between friends and family. Because these agreements are usually founded in casual conversation, they can become points of dissension. In fact, it is the very casualness of verbal agreements that brings an *individual interpretation*; these interpretations may be tinged with self-interest. Personal self-interest creates most of the conflict in interpersonal relationships.

Conflict from these casual interpretations can become quite heated when both parents, of the children, work at jobs outside the home. These jobs, and the demands of getting to and from them each day, directly affects the amount of time available to make dinner, finish homework, take baths, and get ready for the next day.

The parents become severely time crunched. Then, in this time-crunched world, each everyday activity and action is an opportunity for chafing and conflict. Did you say that this week you'd pick up the groceries from the store? Who will make dinner tonight? Who will drop off, and pick up, the kids at school? Do we agree not to bring any cell phones to the table? What are the core values of our family?

One of the ways, which families attempt to mitigate these conflicts and onboard everyone, is by creating written, and posted, family rules. This has the benefit of making how we act, and how we treat each other, overt and obvious. It's hard to have misunderstandings, if the rules are posted on the wall right over the dinner table.

Pinterest is a favorite website for sharing common interests. The Pinteresters create personal boards or "catalogs of ideas." These ideas and interests are created by posting liked and disliked items, on boards that can be shared with others. Pinterest, according to statistics, maintains a 71% female user base, and because of this it is heavily skewed towards fashion, cooking, parenting, and home decoration. Wedding planning boards, though, may be the most popular on Pinterest.

The demographics of Pinterest, which skew female, demographically skew towards under-forty women. And for all the *equality* of the sexes today, wedding planning on Pinterest remains a distinctly female activity. Statistics support this statement about wedding planning: 80% of Pinteresters are women, and they create tens of thousands of boards with ideas about creating a beautiful wedding. Think not? Daily Mail, has an article citing some statistics:

> *One of Pinterest's most popular uses is for wedding planning – especially, it seems, for single women.*
>
> *According to a survey carried out by Mashable and The Knot, an incredible 70 percent of Pinterest users admit to having wedding boards before they are even engaged.*

The numbers aren't lying to us. Women are singularly interested in and love planning weddings. And what's wrong with that? Absolutely nothing in my view. Everything in our world doesn't need to be neutered, degendered; women have every right to love weddings, as much as they want, *IMHO*.

Along with wedding boards and wedding pins, the most popular boards, on Pinterest, are the *family rules* or *house rules* pin boards. Some of the rules make sense, and are good rules for work and life. Here are a few of these rules:

Be Respectful

Be Honest

Be Responsible

Be Grateful

Be Kind

I could post these rules in my office for my employees...and I may... or at home for my family and they'd be great for everyone.

Other rules, on Pinterest, bring a sense of bafflement. Why were they even created?

For example:

Don't Destroy The House

When reading this rule, I was baffled. It reminded me of a scene, in the Will Smith movie, *I, Robot*, from 2004. In the scene, Smith has arrived, at Dr. Alfred Lanning's house, to search it for evidence of his murder. While Smith, as Detective Del Spooner, searches the house, he finds himself being chased down by an oversized, USR demolition machine. The demolition machine is destroying everything in its path, including the house.

But I ask you, *what family* needs a rule saying, *Don't Destroy The House*?

If this is the kind of rule a family has…maybe you shouldn't marry into it. Quietly move on.

Onboarding For Work

Onboarding employees for work is more complicated, and a bit trickier, than the rules for family. Even when we take a significant amount of time in hiring, things can go wrong. Not long ago, I spent weeks interviewing potential employees for a new position in my company. In smaller companies, those with fewer than one-hundred employees such as mine, every employee is crucial to the success of that company. The smaller the company, the more disproportionate affect each employee has on that company functioning smoothly.

Each employee added needs to be a skill fit, as well as a personality fit. In this case, I was sure the right employee had been chosen, but after a short period with us, the employee left, as I noted in the opening to this chapter. The cost to a company when this happens is significant. Not only have you spent time reviewing resumes, and interviewing prospects, but you spend time onboarding the person you've hired, bringing them up-to-speed on the company's method of working, managerial structure, and company core values.

By the time I rehire a new person, for this same role, I'll have spent many, many months on filling a single employee position with my company.

Other reasons onboarding is critical, contemporarily, are the many employment rules, of the government agencies that require adherence, and which change over time. They require continuous monitoring, by your company, so you don't run afoul of them. Compliance, with the legal standards, prevents future difficulties for the company.

And lest we forget, onboarding is vital for the company's culture, and is a critical component of its core values. An employee, who is discordant, doesn't have a team spirit can cause havoc and disruption in a company. Hiring is always difficult, and all companies face various onboarding difficulties.

Newer companies can find that the sheer pressures of growth forces them to hire employees, who…retrospectively…aren't a good hire for the company. As I did. Conversely, larger companies may be scraping the (proverbial) barrel's bottom for available personnel, due to a demand for certain types of skilled employees. This is, especially, true for the large technology companies, who – perpetually – have a difficult time finding new employees. Because of these difficulties, there were rumblings that the larger tech companies had turned to *employee poaching* to fill their software engineer employee requirements. According to the California Employment Law Report:

> *Were Silicon Valley companies artificially keeping wages lower by having an agreement not to poach employees from competitors? This issue came to a head in 2010 when the Department of Justice settled an antitrust case with Adobe, Pixar, Google, Apple, Inuit, and Intel. The DOJ alleged that the companies had an agreement not to poach each other's employees, and that these agreements "reduced their ability to compete for high tech workers and interfered with the proper functioning of the price-setting*

mechanism that otherwise would have prevailed in competition for employees."

In the settlement with the DOJ, the companies agreed to discontinue the use of any agreements that would prevent any company from poaching employees from a competitor.

Hiring Gone Wrong

When an employee is wrong for a company, the employee will never fully onboard; they are either temperamentally mismatched, or because of mismatched skills, the employee is fundamentally not a good fit. This happens more than is thought, as it's not unusual to find that the pressing need for an employee causes the company to overlook, or ignore, flashing signals that the person is a bad fit. The employee is hired anyway, but will probably leave the company soon. Personnel, who are mismatches, will chafe in the company's environment and never click with the other employees.

Another reason, good employees may leave is if they are not provided proper support from the company. To ensure an employee stays with a company, multiple studies indicate that an employee, who is supported through their first three months, will probably stay with the company and be successful in integrating into the social structure. Employees, who aren't guided through this time period, will likely leave the company. Many companies assign each new employee someone within the company, a company companion for the employee, that keeps step with them as they learn the company's ways. This employee is someone for them to have lunch with, ask questions of, and who prevents them from feeling isolated among the larger group of employees, who already know each other.

Customers Need Onboarding, Too

We, sometimes, forget how significant onboarding of customers is to a company. After we've spent so much time creating a product, marketing the product, and getting the product to our customers, it's not unusual for companies to feel they've done their job. They think it's time to celebrate and move on to the next product while the big bucks roll in.

This is exactly the wrong way to think.

At LRT, we've found that customer onboarding is about bringing the customer into the company's system through a step process, which never actually ends. We take a customer, who signed up for our software, through all its functions in a systematic process. Explaining our actual process would take several books. Suffice to say, we've worked very hard to create a team effort, which educates and retains our customers by providing them a sense of total support in using our software. We answer the questions, until the questions are completely answered. And we keep answering them. Forever. As they crop up. Whenever and for as long as our customers have questions, those questions will be answered.

Our ultimate goal, and the goal for anyone providing software, is to provide effortless understanding and use of the software programs. We, as with many companies, are working towards a complete automation system, which teaches our customers the system and paces according to their timelines. We feel it's vital that our users know we have researched, and understood, what their needs are and that the company will stand behind our products. And we make the point, to our clients, that we are available to them, at any time.

Ultimate Onboarding

Overall, onboarding is about a sense of togetherness, cohesion, and agreement with the rules, whether we are at home or work. Social scientists have spent decades studying the issues of organizational cohesion and agree that:

> *Organizational socialization, refers to the mechanism through which new employees acquire the necessary knowledge, skills, and behaviors to become effective organizational members and insiders.*

Onboarding is a never-ending process, as new employees join a company. Employee handbooks, which explain company rules create cohesion and prevent conflict. In the extended family, knowing what the rules are by making them clear, obvious, and understandable, prevents many problems before they start. The family rules clarify the core values and should be created with care, as they will have high impact over time.

Action Step

If your rules are in a closed handbook, or tucked in a drawer, they don't serve as visual prompts for behavior. Companies, as well as families, can post the rules for work or family, on the companies' office wall, or at home, on the kitchen wall. The rules will serve as continuous reinforcements for acting as a team, whether it's the office team or the home team, with the team's rules for interactions and behavior on full display.

Chapter 8

Minimum Viable Product

Do what you can, with what you have, where you are.

Theodore Roosevelt,
American, 26th US President

The story is that Henry Ford, creating the first mass-produced automobile in the early 1900s, proclaimed that the buyers of his automobile could have any color they wanted, as long as it was black. *A minimum-viable-product automobile.* Compare this to today. We walk down any street and see the enormous variation of colors and styles of automobiles that are available to us.

Henry Ford, though, is the role model most software programmers, looking to develop a new product, aspire to emulate. Software products are, initially, created as a *minimum viable product*. You can have it, but you can't have it with all the frills and doodads, so to speak. You can have it as created by the software developers, without any variation. With software, you don't ask, "Do you have it in…?"

Lean and Mean Software Engineering

Of course, we don't know, when we are creating a product, if the public will want to buy it, or not. Software companies begin with a hypothesis about a need they perceive needs filling, do some checking

Minimum Viable Product

on the competitors in the market, maybe hold some focus groups and ask the people in them some questions, and start planning the stages needed to take the project to completion. But ultimately, we're all doing a best-guess scenario. Things may work out great and we become the next Uber or Lyft, or we may crash and burn, watching all our work coming to naught.

Sometimes, we have some real-world influences that push us to create something new. Even if it's a hunch. It may have been a hunch, rather than some hard research on consumer desires that created one of the most detested new products in business history.

A real-world scenario, that went horribly wrong, isn't a software product but a consumer product. In the battle of the fizzy drinks, Coke was holding its own against Pepsi. Consumers, studies showed, liked them both and each company maintained about 50% of the market. However, Coke decided to up the sweetness level of their drink, and to call it *New Coke*. Consumers rebelled. No one had asked for a *New Coke*. No one wanted the *New Coke*, and Coke scrapped its *new* product, returning promptly to the old.

One of the major difficulties in business is we don't know if there is another company creating a similar or competing product. We are concerned that another company's product will compete with our product, and by getting to market slightly sooner, kill our product before it's released. Sometimes, we are aware there is a competing product being developed and this awareness creates significant stress in the process of product development. A company may be required to accelerate the schedule, and bring the product to market sooner than originally planned, and spend more on marketing than they'd planned, so they can stave off the competitors.

New Product Night Terrors

Even if the new product, you are creating, is better than anything else on the market, the new product often brings emotional upheaval.

This is Ben Horowitz's partner at Andreessen Horowitz, Marc Andreessen, explaining the experience of creating a new product, as quoted by Horowitz in his book, *The Hard Thing About Hard Thing*s:

You only ever experience two emotions: euphoria and terror.

Two knee-buckling words, yeah?

When we are creating new software products, as all entrepreneurs do, we invest money and time...the two crucial elements...without an absolute knowledge of return on our investment.

The authors of *Waltzing with Bears*, Tom DeMarco and Timothy Lister, eloquently address the issue of *risk management* in their book. There is, they say, euphoria and terror. "We are routinely expected to work ourselves into a state of believing in a deadline, a budget, or a performance factor, that time subsequently may prove to be impossible."

In product development, whether software or a physical product, we are required to create a baseline minimum value product, a proof of product, *to obtain minimum functionality for a minimum development cost*. Those last few words are everything in software development. Of course, the primary way of ameliorating, these problems in development, is with the *minimum viable product*. Especially in the age of venture capital.

Venture Capital Software Development

The funding from the venture capital community has been manna from Heaven, for startup companies. But these funds usually come with some hard-driving time constraints, and that frequently means allowing sacrifices when it comes to quality, to stability of the product, and letting some software bugs remain in the program.

At LRT, we've felt many of these pressures and sometimes made a sacrifice in quality when the greatest problem facing us was time. We regularly got something done, finished a change to the software as a *minimum viable change*, because we wanted to test the market, even when we knew there were problems that could be fixed if we had more time to spend on the code.

It simply isn't feasible, in software programming, to work out every issue before releasing a product. After all, the issue may not be with the actual software; the problem could be a user's *refusal to read the manual*. Or the problem could be the user's refusal to update *their other software*, so that our software, the new software, will not be running against older software and its problems. Older software may not have the code, which allows the new software to do the job it's designed to do.

Love Your Customers

With a minimum viable product, even more important than the product, may be the company standing behind the product to assist the customer or client. With dedication to servicing their product and a commitment to their core values, a company will build the trust that sustains them for years into the future with their clients, even as the company adds on other products, or adds features to the product that are an additional cost for the customer. Our experience, at LRT, is that clients have no difficulty opening their wallets when they are secure in the knowledge that you provide value and you are always available to assist them with any difficulties, they may encounter.

Team Talk

I have a great team and we do our best to talk openly about any problems that we are aware of and to share our thoughts on possible solutions. And as with any company, LinkResearchTools needs open discussions, on a regular basis. We need to freely share our ideas without holding back any information or thoughts about how our products will work and what will make them successful.

Many companies, and their teams, want to ignore problems. It's easier, at least until the problem is so huge it can no longer be ignored and demands solving. By then, though, the problem can be company threatening, and endangering the ability of the company to continue to exist. If this is the case, it may be too late to solve the problem. This is a primary reason companies find themselves insolvent and going out of business. They have had their heads in the sand, like an ostrich, pretending all is well.

This is not a professional way of solving problems.

At LRT, we had to go through a learning curve and embrace techniques that taught us how to talk to each other about our products and services and the problems we were encountering in the market with them. We had to learn how to present the problems to our employees, without finger pointing and blaming each other, so we could solve them together. Only if this non-accusatory style of solving problems, as a team is embraced, will the problems get solved.

It can be very uncomfortable to discuss a team's problems, whether it is with a single person on the team, or with the entire team, at once. This can be because it is socially unacceptable, if we are having a problem with an employee, to bring up the problem. Or we may be concerned about bringing the problem up, if the person who created it, is one of our managers. We fear creating strife and we fear hurting someone's feelings and we fear being wrong or seen as the agitator. And if we bring up the problem, do we become the disdained messenger? Will we be seen, as the source of the problem? As the famous, and oft repeated, line says: Don't kill the messenger!

An absolute certainty for every business, though, is that the problems don't and won't go away when they are ignored.

If you are a business owner or lead a team for your company, and you are not aware of the problems with the team, then you cannot act and correct the problem. The personnel problems, of a company, roll over and affect the company's products. This is all too true, if the problem requires immediate attention. In the fast-paced world of the internet, we don't have the leisurely schedule of yesteryear to fix our problems.

Before the service economy, and before *software as a service*, became such a large part of the world's economy, businesses could roll up their welcome mat at the end of the day, go home, and open the doors in the morning.

In the current 24-hour world, this doesn't work. When a software program isn't functioning, it isn't functioning for the many people, who depend on it. If you've tried to use an email messaging system that has been down, you've felt the frustration spilling onto the internet, via blogger articles, tweets, and Facebook posts. In the instantaneousness of the internet world, those of us in the software industry know immediately when you are unhappy and when a program is not working for you. And that you want it fixed *right now*. We understand.

Software engineers are quick to respond; we'll jump in and fix the problem, but sometimes...rarely...we may not be able to solve the problem right at that moment. If that's the case, the problem can be evaluated, put on our calendar, and we will push to solve it. This calculated effort will place the expectations of what can be done, and when it should be done, into perspective for our clients.

Closing The Connection

As leaders and business owners, we are sometimes disconnected from our teams and even our clients. And this is one of the biggest problems that occurs in business. We want to be more aware of all the dilemmas faced by our team, but as we juggle the many aspects of running the business, on a daily basis, things can get lost. Tony Hsieh, founder of Zappos, solved this dilemma by changing the relationship between his company and his team.

His solution, ensuring there is connection among the company employees, is trusting his team. Zappos' company core value states that they want their customers for life. To achieve this goal, they reject using pre-written scripts when speaking with the customers. If you're unfamiliar with them, many companies have standardized scripts, appearing on the computer in front of the customer service representative, which tell the representative exactly what to say in varying situations.

Hsieh rejects this method and says, "We want our reps to let their true personalities shine during each phone call so that they can develop a personal emotional connection with the customer." He wants the representatives, above all, to connect and care about the customer.

This kind of personalization and connection can't be achieved with standardized scripted responses.

At Zappos, Hsieh provides, customer service representatives, the decision-making flexibility they need to meet the customer's requests for assistance. This decision-making ability is based on the representatives' knowledge of Zappos' products, and is in keeping with the company's core values. To adapt Zappos' standards, a company should be asking itself these question: Does your team care enough to be sure that the product is meeting the needs of their customers and clients? Do your employees have enough training with your products, to fully assist your customers and clients with their choices?

Ben Horowitz tells it like this. "Companies execute well when everybody is on the same page and everybody is constantly improving. In a vacuum of feedback, there is almost no chance that your company will perform optimally across either dimension. Directions with no corrections will seem fuzzy and obtuse. People rarely improve weakness they are unaware of." With this perspective implemented, Horowitz feels they have a great feedback system in place with their employees.

For most companies, it's great to have a great product. We all want to have the best products we can possibly create and provide them to the market. But the kind of feedback, and the opportunity to serve the clients and customers, which Horowitz and Hsieh have created with their team, is truly invaluable.

Another Kind Of Product

But consider, for a moment, what Zappos or Amazon truly provides their customers and clients. Zappos doesn't make any shoes. Amazon doesn't make any products. Even the "products" they run under the

Amazon banner, *original* movies and shows and books, are brokered out to movie and tv creators and book writers, who create the product. (Nothing wrong with that!)

It does mean, though, that the *minimum viable product* of Amazon is convenience and their amazing service. When you buy something from Amazon your assured it will be delivered and delivered in a timely manner and that it will be as described on the Amazon site. Amazon will 100% stand behind the product, or you can return it for a full refund.

Zappos sells lot of shoes. Running shoes, boots for work and western boots, slippers, and high heels. But the reality is that Zappos is selling Zappos as a minimum viable product. There are lots of places to buy shoes; there is one Zappos. Their minimum viable product is the joy of doing business with the company; their service representatives are the very best, personable and always helpful with any question. Zappos does more though. They don't simply answer questions for customers; the Zappos representatives ask questions about your needs, and their goal is to be an *advocate* for you in finding the right shoes.

To achieve this kind of rapport with customers, every company must receive truthful feedback on their products, no matter how bad that feedback might be. Whatever is hindering the performance of your team, whatever comments or feedback they are hearing from your customers and clients, which indicate there are problems, can't be solved unless you have accurate and necessary information. With a complete picture, of the obstacles or difficulties your clients and customers encounter, your team can move to solving the problems.

As well, any minimum viable product has nothing to offer, if it doesn't offer trust. This is because trust is the basic building block of the minimum viable product. Amazon and Zappos are eminently trusted because of their history of customer relations.

Action Step

Thirty-minute chunks of time are ideal for accomplishing tasks. Thirty minutes is the *minimum viable product* of time. With thirty minutes, you can accomplish more than you might think. Pick a project, any project… clean a closet, weed the garden, or take a walk. Thirty minutes is enough time to give you a sense of accomplishment no matter what task or activity you choose. Enjoy.

Chapter 9

Freemium

Es war wien, war Vienna, wo er alles tat,
er hatte schulden denn er trank.

Lyrics, Rock Me Amadeus
Falco, Austrian, Singer
English translation: It was Vienna, Vienna,
where he did everything,
he had debt because he drank.

Startups are always chasing the sun.

New companies are looking for customers and there are two ways they can obtain them. They either take market share away from an existing company, or they create an entirely new market with a unique product, which brings customers who use…for the first time…this unique product. That said, it's pretty tough to create a product, which is entirely new, which creates its own category and changes the market completely. The computer industry is embedded in everyone's lives, and most of us purchase replacements only when something is broken, or when the upgraded item is irresistible. This means that in some ways, the computer and technology industry is "built out." By this, I mean that the essential elements, computers, smartphones, and the software that run them, have been created. This does not deny that there will be many new products, in the years to come, as technology advances. As I'll discuss in Chapter 14.

So, even though this is generally true, that the *basics* of the technology and computer world, the *basics* of the internet, have been created, it doesn't stop software companies from scrambling to try and find something new or better, to offer consumers. And if they do create a revolutionary software product, some say that the big companies (their names are familiar, so I'll skip naming them here to save myself grief) are actively discouraging these new products from entering the market.

One of the primary ways they do this...*it's said*...is by buying an emerging company and quickly pulling its software from the market. This isn't much different from nature, when the biggest animal drives off the growing, strong youngsters to ensure it retains dominance.

Making A First Appearance

Startups, with interesting products, make themselves known to the market with a *freemium* product. A freemium product is distinguished from free offerings (covered in Ch. 16 Big Data) because they, literally, are giving away their product. Built into the cost of doing business is, a period of time, when the company plans on having zero revenue. The company's goal is a list of customers, sometime in the not-too-distant future, who are habituated to using the company's products and services. Even if they aren't paying anything.

Zero revenue can't go on forever. Zero revenue, as they say in the southern United States, "is a dog that can't hunt." But zero revenue can allow a company to move through a customer-acquisition period. In this period, the company expands and acquires enough customers, a large enough base, so they can move to a pay model. Reaching the pay model level, the company may lose quite a few of their customers. However, they will still have a successful product, because they retain enough customers, who *are* paying for the product.

For example, YouTube started out as a free website. There were tons of great videos, and still are, anyone could watch without paying; this is the freemium product. In essence, YouTube was a television channel, whose channels were comprised, primarily, of amateur videos, similar to the over-the-airways channels of the pre-cable era.

However, YouTube has begun holding back large chunks of content, in the same way that Google cleared out bad websites with *The Penguin*. YouTube has become aggressive about moving copyrighted materials off their site, and ensuring copyright compliance, which provides credibility and an elevated professional standard to their site.

Concomitantly, YouTube is expanding YouTube Red. This is a pay channel, which is a subscription service allowing access to its original programs. According to the New York Times, the subscription service allows viewers to watch videos without advertising interruptions, and to watch the "slate of original programming."

Along with YouTube, it does appear that other websites on the internet, like Hulu, are moving to subscription services. There are a multitude of subscription video services in development, as they are perceived as more profitable than the previous advertising model. For the last thirty years, advertising revenue has been the top performing mode of revenue generation across the web. The success of Netflix, an ongoing, subscription pay service, as the leader in the video services market, is the success model that others are trying to emulate. No doubt many websites attempting this model will be successful, and many will not be successful. Time will tell.

Providing Freemium To Get Customers

At LinkResearchTools, we have extensive information and free training, available on our company website, that fully assists our customers with learning and using our products. All of this material and training is provided without any charge. You know why?

To educate our customers, to keep them learning, to keep them engaged with us. If they don't understand how to use the software, they won't see the value of it and won't pay for the software. And we are in business to make money.

Who wakes up in the morning and gives everything for free to the world? No one.

Business people, like myself, to keep their company in business and their employees paid, must generate revenue, so we can continue to sustain ourselves and provide jobs for our employees. It is capitalism, as Adam Smith explored extensively in *The Wealth of Nations,* which ensures prosperity. Smith wrote, "I have never known much good done by those who affect to trade for the public good."

Significantly, it is the world's richest man, Bill Gates (although various lists quibble it may be Jeff Bezos or Amancio Ortega or Warren Buffett), who wants to do "public good." Bill Gates, whose worth is estimated at almost 88 billion dollars, has the largest philanthropic organization in the world. In 2008, Gates stated he was leaving his fortune to charity, rather than his children. Being really rich lets you be generous.

How Far Freemium

When you find free training, there is always a second thought that should kick in right after you think, "Oh free. Great!"

Spaghetti Code

That thought should be: Why is this free training being offered? It is simply to show you that there is value being offered and that, ultimately, expanded access to the complete bank of training will be exchanged for money? The company is going to offer an upgrade to you, for a fee? Or the free training is being offered, because you are paying for it with something that is valuable to the business, your attention and the possibility that you'll buy from them, soon? There's nothing wrong with that method of enticing you to be a customer.

Many websites offer free information or skill training in exchange for an email address. This is a popular version of freemium on the internet. A business, which you provide your email address, knows that you are the type of customer they want, as you have shown at least an initial interest in their website and products. This is a good deal for both sides. Consumers receive valuable training and information, and a company receives a list of customers it can market to, and who are interested in its products.

Freemiums are found in the non-internet world, as well. Plastic bags are a non-software, consumer freemium. Even though many places where we shop have stopped using them, due to the enormous harm they cause to the environment. The website, Ocean Wild Things, reported on the dead sperm whale found near Mykonos Island. The whale's stomach was filled with plastic bags, non-digestible plastic bags, as well as other kinds of plastics. The report said that when they autopsied the whale to find out what had killed it:

They found a miniature plastic landfill.

The final count was 100 plastic bags in the sperm whale's stomach.

Plastic bags, in the environment, are a travesty and a natural disaster for the environment. Many European countries are on pace to complete a ban plastic bags, as France has done; Italy was on the forefront of banning plastic bags, and most European countries are either in the process of banning them or have greatly limited access to them. China, following suit, has taken steps to greatly limit their use. And news reports indicate that Ireland reported cutting use of the bags by ninety percent, after imposing a fee for each one used. In the United States, California has banned plastic bags, and many cities are in-process of banning them or have banned them, such as Seattle, Portland, Boston, and Austin. This certainly seems like an important step for the environment and our children's future, and therefore, one not to be argued with.

We do want to be cautious that rejecting the elements of our modern life, doesn't become an overzealous, witch-hunt-type-of-agenda. Whether you are selling or buying products doesn't matter. The *virtue signalers* will equally denigrate you on the internet. Sometimes, it seems that the only steps that will assuage the virtue signalers is that we all live naked, sharing one pillow and one blanket, in small communes, eating only berries and roots. Sustainability is intertwined with denigrating being a consumer or a company that produces consumer products.

Anti-consumerism, though, does make valid points. There is no doubt that we need to give more thought to our purchases; landfills are full of stuff that was (we were sure) indispensable, and has been discarded.

Certainly, there are real-world environmental problems that we need to address. But a reasonable balance is necessary. Few consumers care to live a stone-age life; they'll rebel and reject environmental programs if a stringent approach is employed. Enjoying a life of comfortable consumerism is possible, if we continue to monitor and minimize excess waste created from the manufacture of our consumer products.

It's critical to minimize the environmental damages caused by using disposable consumer products. When possible, we can further offset environmental difficulties by choosing higher-quality, longer-lasting consumer goods. Longer lasting products will offset the higher price we pay for them. The environment is our most precious resource, and we have a great, and absolute, responsibility to preserve it for future generations.

Beyond Freemium

Freemium is good if it comes with our personal responsibility that the freemium causes as little environmental degradation as possible. As an example, the freemium of plastic bags clearly violated our responsibility to keep the plastic bags from being tossed into the environment and harming the world's environment for other denizens, like the whales of the planet, and to preserve as pristinely as possible our children's future environment. When we find something truly harmful, such as plastic bags, let's make the effort to change it and lessen the harm as much as possible.

Further, and while the study is still out, *it may be* that a company receives harsher criticism from freemium offers than they do when customers or clients pay for their products. At least, this is the experience of many people, from a wide range of companies, I've spoken with in the last few years. And similarly, just as the environmental advocates have gained traction in banning plastic bags, we may be seeing fewer freemium opportunities from software companies. It may be that freemium is clogging up with internet?

With extensive video clips showing how to use a company's product, instant online conversations with customer representatives that allow the customer to ask any questions they have about the product, and generous refund policies, freemium may be headed for the tech software dustbin. These elements made freemium less necessary, since they provide a stronger information platform for the customer; the customer needs less enticement when they are better informed by the company about its product.

Further, software is no longer a novelty, but an accepted and essential part of our lives. Thus, it may be that software companies are deciding the consumer doesn't need the enticement of freemium to begin a relationship with them. We'll see in the future if this is the position companies are choosing, in presenting their software. Or whether freemium continues to be a popular way of enticing the consumer to try out a product.

For now, LRT and many other businesses will continue providing some services and knowledge for free. But not all of it, of course. And even if you don't use our products, there is learning information, at our site, that is great for expanding your general education, about the internet and links.

As well, at the end of this book, you'll find our resources link, which connects to a wide range of information, including our *7 Golden Rules of Link Building*. With every business and blogger linked to other sites, on the deep-and-wide internet, this is a terrific read about the importance of links. You'll find that the first golden rule is *Build Trust*. My team is dedicated to this core value. There are, of course, many other valuable information resources for you at the resources link.

Freemium Turns Into Payments

And the bottom line is the bottom line. Freemium shows a much higher rate of turning the freemium user into a premium user, a paying user, than the conversion rate from direct advertising efforts. And, once a company has a subscriber in their system, they can raise prices as they feel necessary or simply because they want to. Netflix has raised the subscription price one dollar, for standard service, from $9.99 to $10.99. And so far, there don't seem to be many complaints from subscribers.

Subscription services can be viewed, as the best of all worlds for companies. Rather than being forced to expand their customer base, an increase in the cost of the subscription allows companies, like Netflix, *to revenue increase their customer base*. That is, the company has no need for chasing new customers to create more revenue. They choose, rather, to exploit the customers already purchasing from the company. This isn't a bad thing.

Netflix, for instance, is known for spending extravagantly on original programming; the customers of Netflix enjoy a return on the increased cost of their subscriptions, with fresh and interesting shows, like the popular *Stranger Things*. This neutralizes the sting of the price increase, which might bring complaints if Netflix wasn't providing so much original programming.

Action Step

The fundamental secret in life or work is perseverance. Whether we are expanding a subscription service or making a change in the world, we apply steady movement forward to reach our goals.

Consumers are becoming adamant that the companies be good stewards of the planet. They want to see that businesses are using energy wisely, by creating packaging that is non-polluting to water and soil. This care for the environment is a human core value for all of us, whether we are the consumer of the product or the business creating the product.

As an action step, check a few of the products you use and ask yourself, if the companies you purchase them from, are being good stewards of environmental resources. Are these products using excess packaging? If the answer is yes, maybe it's time to switch to other products, or send a note to the companies asking them to become more aware of environmental issues.

Chapter 10

Hotfix

Dave Bowman: *Hello, HAL. Do you read me, HAL?*

HAL: *Affirmative, Dave. I read you.*

Dave Bowman: *Open the pod bay doors, HAL.*

HAL: *I'm sorry, Dave. I'm afraid I can't do that.*

2001: A Space Odyssey
Stanley Kubrick & Arthur C. Clarke,
American & British, Writers

Software engineers frequently find themselves working on projects that were envisioned by someone else, usually a software project manager. This manager may be long gone, by the time a new programmer joins the project, brought on to write code for it. This means the original concept for the software and its goal, may be unclear, lost to repeated revisions over time.

This will likely mean that the person, who you need to ask the crucial questions, is no longer around. You can't ask them: Why did you write the code like this? Was there a purpose behind writing the code like this? And significantly: Why the hell did you write the code like this?

Coming into an ongoing project, all the software programmer can be sure of, is that there is a *problem* and that the problem must be fixed. As soon as possible.

Pretty code, the code software engineers love to write, is code that looks like beautiful iambic pentameter lines with lovely, lilting feet (groups of syllables in iambic pentameter) cascading gently down the screen. This code can be written later, refined and further refined, to the joy of the software engineer's satisfaction. For the moment, only a hotfix will do to straighten out the "Why the hell did you write code like this?" code.

And Right Now

Hotfixes are for mission critical systems that are not functioning. They, all too frequently, aren't functioning because the release was a way for a developer to test the system, before releasing it widely. Or so says the website, Computer Hope. (Motto: *Free Computer Help Since 1998*)

A very famous television show exemplifies hotfixes, as an immediate requirement, usually because the main characters need the hotfix to solve a predicament and stay alive.

MacGyver was a mid-1980s to early-1990s television program focusing on a secret agent; one who eschewed guns and bullets. Instead, he used his adroit and creative scientific mind to find solutions, as needed when needed, with whatever was at hand. MacGyver might take a clothespin, an abandoned shoelace, a tin can, and a spoon, and from them create *the solution* that got him, and whoever he was rescuing that week, out of their tight spot and away from the bad guys. MacGyver hotfixed every problem he came across, for seven years.

MacGyver could hotfix the problems because he had *thinking versatility*; he didn't see a clothespin, an abandoned shoelace, a tin can, and a spoon, as their individual elements. MacGyver envisioned them together in a completely unique fashion. Together the pieces were the answer he needed for his problem.

This same quality, *thinking versatility*, is an essential component of great software engineers. They can write specific programming languages, and can push them in ways that most programmers wouldn't think of pushing them.

A LinkedIn article presents this idea clearly:

New stuff never comes into the world on its own, it is born when people experiment themselves. The reason many programmers don't have this trait is because they are often fearful of the repercussions or have weak theoretical [sic] foundations. History has always favored the bold, therefore apart from looking for a smart developer, do look for some brave soul.

If a company won't face up to what needs to be done, the problems snowball.

This evaluation of Myspace and Facebook, from the Massachusetts Institute of Technology website, is clarifying and should inspire entrepreneurs to view change, as sometimes very necessary:

The success of this technique becomes exceptionally clear when comparing the recent social network giants, Myspace and Facebook. The issue with Myspace was not necessarily feature creep, but instead that it refused to update its user experience. It felt that any changes to the "user profile" page would cause its users' profile designs to break and result in a significant loss of membership. Keep in mind though, altering a profile design on Myspace effectively requires users to hack HTML and CSS into the "About Me" section of their profile. Rather than building a profile customization tool embedded in Myspace to automate this, the company remained static and left their questionable user experience standing.

Everyone knows what happened next.

Hotfixes can be the difference between a company surviving and thriving, or becoming a Silicon Valley cautionary tale. Software engineers have to stay ahead of the problems, and live to write another day, by using hotfixes when they are necessary.

Hotfixes For Ergonomics

The era of computers brought accompanying mental and physical demands, never before seen in offices. These demands provoked decidedly unhealthy responses to the "artificial" environment of working at computers for many hours a day. Or, as is frequently the case for software engineers, many hours *into* the night, day-after-day until the project is complete. These mental and physical demands are draining and exhaust us, whether we are working at computers at a company office or at a computer in our home office.

Chiropractors are seeing more patients for back problems resulting from sitting incorrectly. Ophthalmologists are seeing patients for their eye strain from the unnatural light of digital screens. Orthopedic surgeons are seeing patients, who have carpal tunnel wrist problems, from hunching their wrists over a mouse or keyboard.

The response to these ergonomic problems has been a plethora of devices designed to create a healthier and more comfortable workspace. Luckily for office and home workers, manufacturers have responded to the ergonomic difficulties with solutions for any part of your body strained and causing pain.

There are keyboards that tilt to any angle, which feels best for us, such as the Uncaged Ergonomics Drawer with Negative Tilt. This keyboard moves up and down, while sitting or standing, and the keyboard allows for a negative tilt.

Why, you might ask, would anyone want a negative tilt? It's a counterintuitive design, isn't it? But as it turns out, it's the best design for human joints. Here's a review from All Things Ergo:

> *Ergonomists have long decried positive tilt, as a menace to correct wrist position. In recent years, they have begun to favor not just zero-tilt, but negative tilt as a beneficial position. Think about it: Are your hands more comfortable bent back as if you were waving someone off, or relaxed out in front of you, arms angled slightly down?*

Along with keyboards, there are *risers*. These are placed on the tops of our desks, to make our desks function as *standing desks*. You may find, as many people have found, that spending time at the computer becomes easier if you alternate between standing and sitting. Workers find this creates an easier, less stressful way to work over the course of the day. Popular risers, include the Stand-Up Desk Store Air Rise Pro-Height Adjustable Standing Desk Converter or the Smonet Sit to Stand Desk Riser Converter, as examples. (All ergonomic design companies seem disinclined to use less than ten-to-twenty words in their product descriptions.)

For a fully-convertible ergonomic desk, the Evodesk Pro™ has automatically adjustable height positions, with the press of a button. And the manufacturer even provides an *ergonomic edge* on the desk, if you choose it.

And you can choose from a range of items designed for adding to your chair comfort. The Aloudy Ergonomic Memory Foam Chair Armrest Pad for Elbows and Forearms is designed for keeping elbows from hitting the hard plastic of most common desk chair arms.

Nor do the ergonomic designers ignore our feet. The Eureka Ergonomic Tilt Adjustable Footrest with Massage Surface, from Designa, is one of the many footrests available for under the desk. These are designed for foot stimulation, for keeping the blood moving in your feet, and letting you massage your feet, while sitting. (Interestingly enough, the brilliant scientist, Tesla, was said to have a habit of moving his feet up and down to encourage blood circulation.)

In addition, there are ergonomic floor mats. You can choose a simple one for around thirty dollars or a more expensive and intriguing one like the TerraMat Standing Desk Mat. This mat is a *topographically-designed comfort standing fidget mat* (company's description!), which was created as an anti-fatigue mat for using with stand-up desks and standing workstations. This mat is from CubeFit.

Or you could choose the Ergohead Standing Desk Mat-Not-Flat Anti Fatigue Mat For Stand Up Desk, whose benefits…according to the company…include: Massaging, Large Space for Movement, Pebbled Skin, and Patent Pending Standing Positions That Encourage Movement for Health. (Please note all descriptions of these products are taken directly from the manufacturers, and as such, may lack a grammatical perfection.)

Some of these hotfixes for the wear-and-tear of our computer-world life, for spending too many hours in front of a computer screen, might seem a bit much. At first glance. After all, a desk mat that has *massage* areas?

But since sitting for long periods...at a computer...has been established, as causing many of the major health problems of our time, we need to do all we can to alleviate them. These problems include spine inflexibility, poor circulation in the legs, soft bones, and strained necks. Thus, thinking about creating the best workplace environment, and then taking the necessary steps to keep our offices in line with our body's ergonomics, hotfixing our office for health, is vital in today's stressful office environments.

These hotfixes may turn out to be more important than we think they are at this time. There is, yet, to be a generation of workers, who have spent their entire life in front of computers, while at work. Decades may pass before we see the health difficulties that are associated with this change in our lifestyle or workstyle. There may be an entirely new and different set of health ills categorized and which are directly related to computers.

These ergonomic hotfixes for the computer life are worth trying. Your health, of course, is with you whether you are at home or at work!

Action Step

Human beings are made for *movement*. If you've attended the Olympics, or watched the Olympics when it's on television, you see athletes pushing their bodies as far as they physically can, to the most demanding point that muscles can be pushed, as they prepare for and take part in the events. The accomplishments and athleticism of the athletes is simply astounding.

Of course, we are *sitting,* while we are watching these accomplished athletes. In fact, the natural course of our lives, contemporary life is consumed with sitting. We sit at work and then go home and sit, whether it's watching a television show, Netflix, or being a couch potato. Sitting is the singular activity of our time, defining our lives, unfortunately for us, since sitting ruins our health. Our bodies are jointed, for a reason. That reason is that we are structured to be moving, to walk, to run, to dance, to hop and skip. Our bodies are (should be treated as) perpetual motion machines.

The choice is easily made to add some movement into your life. Home treadmills have become popular due to their low cost, or you can walk around the house several times. Many people do walk around their house during the commercials on television. Jumping jacks and a jump rope require a very tiny clear area for you to participate in these movements. Most offices have plenty of open space where you can do a few jumping jacks or use a jump rope.

Or you can turn on some music and dance with your spouse or with your children. Children will always dance, with the least little bit of encouragement. They don't feel a need to know steps or feel a need to look good. They dance when the music starts and stop when the music ends. We should follow their lead.

The important thing, no matter what you do, is to move so that oxygen circulates through your muscles. Without oxygen moving through your body, the carbon dioxide builds up leading to decreased ability of your muscles and accelerates their decay. Indicators from medical studies show that by moving your body, you prevent plaque from building up in your brain; a major cause, it's believed, of early senility. The way you add movement into your life is not critical. What is critical is ensuring that you *are* adding *movement* into your life. Keep moving is the first guideline for health.

And a *hint* for men. Wallets, in the back pocket, will throw off the alignment of the spine, while you are sitting. Remove your wallet when sitting, to a convenient place, when you are working. A place you'll remember to pick it up from when you are ready to leave work and head for home.

Chapter 11
Waterfall Optimism

Don't bend; don't water it down; don't try to make it logical; don't edit your own soul according to the fashion. Rather, follow your most intense obsessions mercilessly.

Franz Kafka, Austrian, Author

In our best version of life and work, we make plans, follow the plans, and celebrate when we cross the finish line. Software developers have come to call this process the *waterfall process* of developing software. This process moves through the following steps: Conception, Initiation, Analysis, Design, Construction, Testing, Implementation, and Maintenance. If you've ever seen pictures of Niagara Falls, located in the United States, or Victoria Falls, located in Zimbabwe, the analogy is obvious. Waterfalls go one direction, flowing down over their various levels until they reach the beautiful, clear, bright-blue pool below, where lush, green flora abounds and no one else is around. Paradise found.

The waterfall process is the direct opposite of a *death march* (recall Chapter 5). In the waterfall process, the planning has been astute, extraneous steps omitted, and the timeline is accurate and reachable. Some evaluations of the waterfall process compare it to *Agile software development*, which is said to "focus on smaller work areas, overhead becomes less, and the project costs considerably less than when using the waterfall method."

A Flow To The Finish

There's some quibble involved there. But in a world where the number of options, for development of products whether digital or physical, has exponentially increased, a waterfall process gives us a direct flow to the finish. And achievements can't be counted unless they are finished.

One of the most motivational authorities on achievement is Grant Cardone, who says, "Be a person that finishes what you begin!" Grant Cardone is the author of five books, and one of the top trainers for self-improvement, motivation, and sales training in the world. He's a passionate and powerful competitor, with little patience for whining. His books should be on everyone's shelf.

Do You Need A Plan?

Not everyone believes in following a plan. In a kind of fly-by-the-seat-of-your-pants plan, *Rework* authors, Jason Fried and David Heinemeier Hansson, suggest the following:

> *Why don't we call plans what they really are: guesses…When you turn guesses into plans, you enter a danger zone. Plans let the past drive the future. They put blinders on you. "This is where we're going because, well, that's where we said we were going." And that's the problem: Plans are inconsistent with improvisation… The timing of long-range plans is screwed up too. You have the most information when you're doing something, not before you've done it. Yet when do you write a plan? Usually, it's before you've even begun. That's the worst time to make a big decision…Decide what you're going to do this week, not this year. Figure out the next most important thing and do that. Make decisions right before you do something, not far in advance.*

Right. While their book, *Rework*, contains many interesting and good ideas about creating and running a business, this idea isn't one of their best. For example, imagine that you are deciding to visit relatives, who live 500 miles away. Why not simply get in the car and drive? Answer: Because a plan and a map (on your smartphone or...how quaint...on paper) will get you there. Without a plan and a map, you could end up... who knows where?

Plans and maps are critical to success, which isn't to say they can't be reimagined, moderated or changed. As personal life circumstances or world events or the business world change, these changes can and will influence the course that we've chosen, and it may be necessary to moderate the plan. No course of action should be considered, as written in stone. Adaption and adjustment are two of the most valuable skills, in business and life. Don't hesitate to use these two vital skills.

Plans Are Goals

Plans are important for many reasons, not the least of which is that they provide us a motivation for moving from where we are to where we want to be, aka *the goal*! Optimism doesn't simply exist, as some kind of amorphous floating cloud, but has an origin point. The plan moves us from the origin point to the completion point. With the series of steps laid out, the plan conveys a sense of forward momentum and purpose, assuring us that what we want is achievable. And when we see that the plan is achievable, optimism is fanned.

As Grant Cardone tells us in his book, *The 10X Rule: The Only Difference Between Success and Failure*, "The concepts of goal setting, target attainment, and taking action are not taught in schools, management classes, leadership training, or weekend conferences at the Four Seasons."

In other words, it's necessary that we learn to achieve our goal and our goal can only be achieved with a plan. This is not to say that plans don't change or can't be modified along the way, and this point should be obvious. But beginning, with even a generously roughed-out plan, will get you further than *no plan* or a plan that isn't more than a couple of scrawled thoughts on a bar napkin.

To reach our goals, Cardone recommends building the "discipline of taking massive action." And, because much of the training Cardone's conferences and books provide is targeted to sales professionals, he reiterates a study, which attests that "80% of sales to businesses are made on the fifth sales call."

This could mean different things, however. It could mean that the sales are highly-complex ones, with each one costing the business tens of thousands of dollars. If so, the sales professionals could be required to make their way through various steps, with the purchasing company, before the purchase is allowed. It could mean that the sales professional isn't good at their job; many sales professionals should be in a different field or profession. Selling to others is an art and there are a very few, who have the true gift of being a sales professional. Although it is certainly true that sales can be learned. To that end, continuous sales training is essential, as evidenced by the popularity of Cardone's training programs.

If the sales professionals haven't been properly trained by their company, the salesperson will not be able to connect with their customers and succeed in selling the product or service. If the company hasn't invested in training for the sales team, the sales professionals will not be fully trained on the benefits of their product or service. As such, they won't be able to convince, the person they are selling the product or service to, that their company should purchase the product.

Waterfall Optimism

If a company has provided adequate sales training, the sales person still won't be effective, if they aren't optimistic about making the sale. A sales professional can have all the training a company is able to provide and be so negative that they self-defeat, before they've knocked on the door.

Optimism Beats Self-Defeating Behavior

Self-defeating behavior is the opposite of optimistic behavior. And I don't believe that anyone is born self-defeating; people learn that trait. Lots of studies have been done, throughout the years, on self-defeating behavior and what causes it. The studies conclude there is no genetic evidence for a pessimism or "desire for defeat" gene. Grant Cardone rails against those who tell us we "can't." He says, "Who told you I can't do that? Where is the rule or protocol that says you cannot do this? Who is giving you this kind of suppressive advice?"

And he is exactly right. If you demand that any "can't" be justified, be qualified, and be shown as an absolute (i.e., You can't jump across the ocean!), you'll find the "can't" is based on the failure of someone else's choice in the past and which they are projecting into your "reality." That person, who failed, is someone without your abilities, your talent, and your desire for success. For that person, the "can't" is the reality. But for you, and your reality and goals, you can reject the "can't," which others with less desire and drive, try to project onto you.

Sales always involves a goal and to have a goal requires optimism. Optimism is buttressed and sustained by a diligently, thought-out plan.

The Sustenance Of Optimism

Optimism is the mother's milk of a great plan, providing the sustenance to keep moving towards the goal and working through the steps of the plan, the waterfall moving us naturally forward. This is not to deny that we can be too optimistic. Just as a great plan, without optimism, is going to fail. Optimism can't overcome a plan based on false assumptions, or the need for adequate resources and skills to complete the plan. The Panama Canal had its start with one country, France, in 1881, but due to the financial corruption associated with the Canal's management in France, wasn't completed until 1914, ten years after the United States took over the project.

One of the few billionaires in the world, Peter Thiel, cites optimism, in *Zero To One: Notes on Startups, or How to Build the Future*, as the stock-in-trade of great achievements, like the Panama Canal. He writes that the United States, "has always been home to the world's most far-seeing optimists." The United States, as Thiel points out, has been the driver of its own gigantic infrastructure designs, such as the public drinking water systems and the highway systems of the country. It is, of course, the United States, which has landed men on the moon. So far, the sole country that has achieved this feat.

To believe you can send men to the moon and bring them back? That is the epitome of optimism. Optimism will never, though, overcome a lack of committed money, natural resources, and human talent. When the United States decided to land a man on the moon, the full resources of the United States were harnessed to achieve that goal. A lackluster commitment, or less than complete dedication to the safety of the astronauts, would have surely meant failure in achieving this goal.

In the business world, we sometimes bite off more than is possible to achieve. We know what we want and what our goal is, but with the resources we want to commit to complete a project, it probably can't be achieved. Or we push endless resources at a project, and become mired down in the logistics of the project, and never start the project.

In the past, I've seen software managers, who thought they could write 1000s of pages of requirements with thousands more pages of detailed specifications, and who believe the pages would coalesce into a plan. Then, after three years of developing this "plan," the managers turn it over to the software engineers, who are told to begin the coding of the software. Unfortunately, the world has been moving along for three years and the plan is completely obsolete. In this case, there's been a huge waste of time and money. The two cardinal sins of business.

Ben Horowitz faced this problem with bringing the browser, Netscape, to market. "At Netscape, we went public when we were fifteen months old. Had we started six months later, we would have been late to a market crowded, by that time, with thirty-seven other browser companies." Further, he notes, "Even if nobody beats you to the punch, no matter how beautiful your dream, most employees will lose faith after the first five or six years of not achieving it."

In his book, *The Hard Thing about Hard Things*, he, also, recognizes that money burn endangers the ability to access the other resources the company needs for its success. Without money, there will be no employees, no office space, no anything, and the company will fail. Burning time is burning money.

Rather than looking at our plans and our goals, as either set in stone, or created by the seat-of-our-pants as we go along, a *comprehensive plan* accompanied by an enormous jolt of optimism is the best bet. Add to that, reevaluation when necessary, based on changes in the world, and the goal can and will be achieved.

Action Steps

> *People who abandon positive attitudes might not even be aware of market recovery when it occurs due to the blindness they've adopted and the poor work ethic they've made into a habit.*
>
> Grant Cardone, *If You're Not First, You're Last: Sales Strategies to Dominate Your Market and Beat Your Competition*

Action Step One

Pessimism and negative thinking, or negative self-talk, is a habit. And it is a contagious habit; complainers prefer the company of other complainers and if you aren't a complainer, the choice of pessimists will be to turn you into one of them. Psychologist Travis Bradberry offers this advice to protect yourself from the contagion of negativism.

First, set limits with the complainer by listening to them, as briefly as possible. Second, offer some support with a step or steps they can take to solve the problem. And third, change the subject of conversation or, as a last step, physically remove yourself from their vicinity, if the complainer isn't showing real interest in correcting the problem. Misery, as the saying goes, loves company, but you don't have to be the company!

Action Step Two

I had returned from a trip to Dubai, and while flying on the plane, I was thinking about negativity and its effect on myself, my family, and my business. After arriving home, my daughter and I began playing a game where we would be positive for a while, say fifteen minutes. At first, she complained...how ironic!...about being positive. But I've noticed that after we play the game, we are more positive for the rest of the evening.

Instituting *positive segments of time,* for your family or business each day, as a means of creating harmony and optimism costs absolutely nothing. Choose, an hour or a couple of hours, when a positive perspective is required, and nothing negative can be brought up or said. We call this *positive mode.* It seems to have a "halo" effect and spills over into the rest of the day, long after we've stopped actively thinking about being in positive mode.

My belief is that keeping a positive attitude, really does change our view of the world and give us the energy to achieve more things. This is not to say that I don't call out things that are not right, things that I perceive are wrong or ridiculous. And it doesn't mean that those around you will appreciate this change in your perspective. The naysayers will try to pull you back into their negative circle of influence. This is to be expected.

At first, you'll need to make a concerted effort, and be consciously aware this is happening, and protect yourself from the naysayers. Soon, though, you'll find you develop an immediate intuitive awareness they are nearby, and you'll move out of the vicinity of their possible influence, without even thinking about it.

Chapter 12

24/7

This above all: to thine own self be true.

William Shakespeare,
Poet-Playwright-Dramatist, English

No one knows, as we wake each day, what may have changed in the world, while we slept. Every day, the headlines on news sites changes, telling us what is happening with our fellow humans. When we read the headlines, we can count on many of them referring to the ongoing competition for business supremacy. Business news moves the world.

There have been ruthless attempts to stamp out competition, to level the playing field, to deny capitalism. This can be done with a heavy enough hand, as Mao's revolution or the Bolshevik revolution has shown us. But, *eventually*, a desire to be entrepreneurial, to take market share…whether it's having the best carrots at the farmer's market or the fastest browser, reignites and revitalizes capitalism. Competition, it seems, cannot be killed. It's been tried, as happened with Mao's revolution and the Bolshevik revolution, but famine and disease usually kill communism. Capitalism always wins. Sooner or later.

The Other Kind Of Revolution

Social revolutions are, usually, temporary. A business revolution, though, changes our world forever. Marc Benioff, CEO and Founder of Salesforce, wrote the book, *Behind the Cloud: The Untold Story of How Salesforce.com Went from Idea to Billion-Dollar Company-and Revolutionized an Industry*.

In the book, he says, "Keep in mind that the landscape is always changing; you must always examine what's working, evolve your ideas, and change the way you do things." In creating Salesforce, the crux of his vision was to move from software delivered on physical materials, such as a computer disc, to *software as a service*. And in fact, in only a couple of decades, the computer industry has almost entirely moved to software as a service. This is a business revolution.

No longer is the consumer/client required to order and wait for delivery of physical discs in the mail, or go to a retailer, wait in line to pay, return to the office with the discs and load them to their computers. At that point, the software was accessible and able to be used by the purchaser.

Software, as a service, has brought instantaneous access, as well as the infamous idea of dipping into the consumer/client's pocket *forever*, with monthly charges. The advantages, though, make an argument against software as a service, difficult. The user is advised of updates to the software, with a quick push notification or an email. Then, with a couple of clicks, the user brings all their software programs up-to-date via an internet connection.

In 1995, when Bill Gates' first book, *The Road Ahead*, was published, this kind of downloading, and the extent of the computer industry and the interconnectedness of websites, was only a possibility. To realize how far the world has evolved, it's interesting to take a retrospective peek at where Gates thought we were headed, and where we have been.

It's daunting to read, in his introduction, an acknowledgment that begins, "The past twenty years have been an incredible adventure for me."

Gates was writing that line in 1995. But he is writing about the two decades that began in 1975, more than forty years ago. Gates dropped out of Harvard University, to begin Microsoft, with Paul Allen. Turning all their attention to the new company, Gates and Allen went to work developing a market for Microsoft's computer software. He was influenced by his reading of the magazine, *Popular Electronics,* which published its description of the computer as a *household item*. In January of 1975, the magazine proclaimed:

The Home Computer Is Here

For many years, we've been reading and hearing about how computers will one day be a household item...high chip costs would have made this a most expensive toy...with the availability of the Intel 8080...the highest-performance, single-chip processor available...the Altair 8800 offers up to 65,000 words of memory, 256 inputs and outputs simultaneously.

The Altair priced in at "under $400." And for that price, you'll notice there was neither a screen nor a keyboard, included in the description. There were (see below list of included items) blinking lights, *an electronic Morse code*. The blinking lights were interpreted and used to understand the Altair's output, to decode the message.

The *Popular Electronics* article waxed eloquent. "The era of the computer in every home – a favorite topic among science-fiction writers – has arrived!"

The article goes on to list each, and every part of the Altair 8800, including the disc capacitor, the 8080-central processing unit, LED1 to LED36 – Panel-type, red light-emitting diode, and the spring-loaded, momentary-action miniature toggle switch, and metal case. Sold as a complete kit, the purchaser wanted to know exactly what was included and *Popular Electronics* was thorough in presenting a highly-detailed list. Then, for sales momentum, they add, "Fundamental programming concepts are simple enough to master in a relatively short time." They qualified this statement by adding, "However, to become an efficient programmer requires years of experience and a *large amount of creativity.*"

The Internet of Things To Come

The conclusion of the article provides fascinating points, about the internet of things to come. It lists "a small sampling of the thousands of possible applications for the computer. The Altair 8800 is so powerful, in fact, that many of these applications can be performed simultaneously." Some of those applications included being used as a calculator, a ham station, an intrusion alarm system, a digital clock, an automobile test analyzer, to autopilot planes and boats, as a brain for a robot, as a pattern-recognition device, to control heat and air conditioning, and as a signal analyzer.

The article ends by assuring the reader, of a description of the operating of the computer and that "some sample programs," as part 2, will be available in the next month's issue of *Popular Electronics*. If you take another look at that list, you'll see how prescient *Popular*

Electronics was in imaging how the computer would influence business and our lives. Each, and every one of those applications, is virtually common today. We use the computer programs, *Popular Electronics* listed, for the functioning of modern society.

Today Computers Are Everywhere

We have reached the point of technology ubiquitousness; computers are everywhere, managing every aspect of our lives, and as we carry *smartphones*, technology is with us, *always and everywhere*. This creates stress in our lives, no matter how much we might appreciate being able to connect with our family or order some milk delivered to the door.

The stress, of an *immediate and always on world*, is felt deeply when you run a business, as the first rule of any business is the "buck stops with me." As much as I might like to take a day off or a week off from being the boss, while I own the company, while I am the boss, there is little chance of that happening.

As an owner, there are many responsibilities, some of them are to your employees and some of them are to your customers. But of the two responsibilities, unless the customer is your priority, you will lose the customer and your revenue stream.

If you've ever heard from an irate customer with a problem, you know they don't care if it's five minutes before time-to-go-home for you and the employees. If a company is your client, and selling on the internet, up-and-running 24/7, they demand and require that whatever is broken and whatever needs fixing, be fixed immediately, if not sooner.

Businesses will vary on how they choose to accommodate this kind of challenge. It's a mission critical challenge that requires resources and manpower and extensive ongoing planning to ensure positive outcomes when facing these difficulties.

The Internet Will Get Bigger

Statistically, some of the top pundit "technologists" estimate that we are at a twenty-percent build out of the internet. This means 80% of the internet is still to be developed. Hard to imagine, isn't it?

But as the saying goes, where there's a problem there's an opportunity. My company, in fact, is focused on these kinds of *opportunities*. As the internet expands, companies will find many backlinks connected to them they didn't approve. These links connect them to websites, which they would rather not associate with. Sometimes these connections are not harmful; they are inadvertent connections. But, sometimes they are malicious, and can cause the business significant harm. Regardless, it's necessary to know who you are associating with on the internet. Our software is assisting businesses, in keeping their associations with other website and the links on the internet which connect back to them, positive and beneficial to them.

A Business Owner's Worries

You might ask, what do business owners worry about the most?

With the internet, every business is constantly under threat of losing market share. This is true for us at LRT, as well. We are very aware that there is another business, or many other businesses that would love to take market share from us. And we worry about it.

Even though we work hard at being the best, if the code for our software is not up-to-date, if we aren't always working towards doing the best job for our clients, we will lose market share. To meet this challenge, we work long hours. Software, and providing it to clients, is a challenging business.

And if we lost market share, the cascade of events that would follow could devastate my team and myself. I worry that losing market share might lead to laying off an employee or employees. Of course, before that step would be taken, my choice would be to tighten other aspects of the business, and see where we might save funds so that employees aren't laid off.

Because of these business worries, my team and I are…in effect…a 24/7 team. Yes, we go home at the end of the day, and we take off weekends and holidays, but if something goes wrong with the software and our clients don't feel it is working properly no matter the reason, our clients will look elsewhere for their software if we don't have it fixed immediately. If not sooner. My team understands, as well as I do, that the pace of the world has changed, and we must flow with that change and adapt to it.

This 24/7/global world demands attention on the schedule of our clients, not our schedule. Even when LRT attends the annual SEOktoberfest in Munich, Germany, enjoying the beers and bratwursts, our software, serving our clients, must function at its highest levels, 24/7. Today, tomorrow, and the day after tomorrow.

Action Step

The pressure on all of us to be present all the time, as demanded by the internet's always-on presence, can be wearing. One way to alleviate this pressure is to use grocery delivery services, as much as possible. Even substituting delivery, every other time you might go to the store, is a huge time savings.

More and more companies are beginning to offer delivery service. They are giving us a gift in a time-crunched world, and a service which is essential when we have colds or don't feel well enough to get to the store. Take advantage of the delivery service, and use the time savings for other things more meaningful to your life.

Chapter 13

Garbage In Garbage Out

*Seek not good from without: seek it within yourselves,
or you will never find it.*

Bertha von Suttner, Austrian, Pacifist Author,
1st Sole Woman Nobel Prize Winner 1905
(Madame Curie was the first woman winner
of the Nobel Prize with her husband, Pierre Curie, 1903)

If you've ever bought a t-shirt, washed it, and pulled it out of the dryer to find it has completely fallen apart, you've experienced the phenomena of *garbage in garbage out*. A manufacturer, who uses cheap materials is using garbage for their input, and can...by default...only have garbage as an output. The one place, that garbage going in results in something that is not garbage coming out, is with gardening. Gardeners love garbage. Gardeners turn garbage, lawn clippings, and kitchen waste into compost, and after distributing the compost into their garden, end up with beautiful, tasty vegetables for the table.

But this isn't a gardening book.

The Dumb Beast Among Us

For software programmers, garbage in becomes a significant problem. Computers, because they are *dumb beasts*...in many ways...don't care if you have *input garbage*. Artificial intelligence may overcome some of these problem, and be able to correct bad input garbage. But when considering, the endless permutations possible, in entering information into a computer, we are in for a long run before the difficulties, with garbage in, are solved.

The computer is not and can be, no better than the programs, created by the programmers, which process the information, which is input. Take another look at that sentence and you see the potential for two places where the system fails. Garbage in may fail because the software program being used has been badly written, i.e., a great program may *overcome bad information* input. Or, garbage in may fail because the *input information* is bad information.

In the case of the input information, the computer will run its program and attempt to provide you the output, regardless of how bad the information you've put in. The computer will crunch and crunch away, trying to arrive at "the answer," because that is what it is designed to do.

Inversely, no matter how great the information you put in is, even if Einstein was putting in the information, if the software program is poorly written, the output will be inadequate or wrong or simply make no sense whatsoever. You'll get gobbledygook. It might look like it makes sense at first, but the information won't hold up to scrutiny and rigorous testing.

Computers are *beasts* of analysis and logic: If the premises (inputs) are faulty, the answers (outputs) will be faulty.

One of the best examples of this, for anyone to understand easily, is the 1983 movie, *WarGames*, with Matthew Broderick. According to IMDB (Internet Movie Database), David Lightman, a teenage computer whiz, stumbles into a backdoor to the US supercomputer that maintains control over the nuclear weapons. Unaware of this, he begins playing the games that are on the computer. However, these games are used to teach the computer *game theory*, a way to find a win in the "game," no matter the scenario.

When he begins playing Global Thermonuclear War, with the computer, he isn't aware that the computer believes…due to the garbage input…that the US is under attack by foreign powers. Later realizing the mistake he's made, as the computer is playing the game of nuclear warfare to win, he convinces the computer that the information is faulty. With this information, the computer chooses to end the game, and not destroy the world with global thermonuclear warfare.

Garbage input is easily seen in our daily lives. As my t-shirt example and the *WarGames* example illustrates, when we choose garbage input, there can only be one result. Humans are the guardians at the gate, and must apply rigorous standards to keep the input clean and accurate, if we want useful results.

Controlling Garbage In

In my own life, because I travel frequently, which results in changing time zones, I found my sleep patterns were being disrupted. I was experiencing a constant feeling of sleepiness. This feeling of sleepiness, which is a result of sleep deprivation from disrupting the body's circadian rhythm, is so common, we refer to it as *jet lag*.

Because my travel is primarily for business, as I speak frequently at conferences, I feel the effects of jet lag sharply. This could be a problem, since I need to be fully alert, when giving a presentation and answering audience questions.

I'd heard about various vitamins that can mitigate the stress effects of flying, and began some research on supplements. In reviewing supplements and thinking about adding them to my diet, I ended up scrutinizing my eating patterns. What we eat, when we fly, is more important than we think. This is because, while flying has become an everyday event, it isn't natural or normal.

Flying should be perceived, as the stressful event it is, no matter how frequently or infrequently we fly. Not a single one of us has wings, although evolutionary biology indicates we might have had them in the past. Because we don't have wings, our bodies are designed to live on the earth's surface, not at an airplane's flying height of 32,000 to 40,000 feet, above the ground. Further, we're not designed to move at the 500-miles-per-hour an airplane travels.

To solve my travel stress, I added supplements of vitamin C, which many consider the most crucial vitamin for human health. And I order extra vegetables with my meals while traveling, replacing carbohydrates with the vegetables. Along with more vegetables, I reduce how much meat I eat, as meat is harder to digest than fruits and vegetables. Lastly, alcohol places a strain on our kidneys, as it is a diuretic. To counter this effect, I add bottles of water and other non-sugary liquids to my diet, such as tea with a bit of honey, when I've had beer or wine the night before.

Of course, everyone should check with their doctor before adding any supplements to their diet, even something as innocuous as vitamin C. And it may be a great idea to check with your doctor about the effect of time changes on your prescription schedule. If you have scheduled travel, you'll need to time your prescriptions to make them effective, and not inadvertently take them too close together or too far apart, as you fly.

Another problem, I've faced in traveling, is breathing airplane forced air. Airplane air circulates every germ and virus of all the passengers of the plane you're flying on. During cold and flu season, this becomes a critical health problem. Even if another passenger doesn't have obvious symptoms of a cold or flu, they can still be passing on cold and flu causing germs into the airplane's oxygen system.

My solution for *garbage in* air is to not put *garbage* food into my system. Eating high-quality organic food (waiting to eat, if necessary) is important for everyone's health, especially when traveling.

Sorry to say this, but airline food is frequently over-cooked, before being boarded onto the plane, depleting the last fragments of vitamins from any vegetables. It's then heated in a microwave, at the last minute, before serving to the passengers, which is why there are so many jokes about airline food.

Clearly, airlines have significant constraints when trying to feed their passengers. After all, they certainly can't be expected to have full kitchens and chefs on the planes, cooking scratch meals at 30,000 feet in the air.

To alleviate the problems of nutritionally-deprived airline meals, we are much better off paying a little more for pesticide-free fruits and vegetables in our daily lives. We can choose quality, free-range chickens and grass-fed beef, rather than consuming food, which doesn't offer the nutritional value and health benefits of organic. This allows our bodies to "bulk up" on vitamins and good nutrition for the stressful times we encounter, like flying. This is the essence of the popular paleo diets. Eat quality simple food, as close to the source as we can.

We can make eating organic easier, since it's sometimes considered inconvenient and expensive, by using the farm-to-table movement and CSA, Consumer Supported Agriculture. This system gives us the opportunity for a pivotal change in how we buy our fruits and vegetables. With CSA subscriptions, each person or family that signs up, receives a box of fruits and vegetables fresh from the farm, with regularly scheduled deliveries. This schedule coordinates to the natural growing cycle of the farm. CSA subscriptions aren't available everywhere, but have become popular, and are in a definite growth pattern. You can check on the internet to find one in your own area.

The Source Is The Suspect

The internet is the single greatest purveyor of garbage in garbage out; a significant amount of news on the internet is being referred to as *fake news*, meaning the news should be considered "source suspect." Unfortunately, fake news and fake information is not a new phenomenon, even though we think it is. Snake oil salesmen, whether they are selling "information" or elixir, have been around for millennia.

The website, The Onion, which publishes satirical, fake news, as a matter of course, is a well-loved site. Here are a couple of their headlines:

Bird Wouldn't Have Landed On Ledge If It Had Known Everyone Would Make It Into Whole Big Thing

The article relates the bird's perspective:

"Gawd, if I'd realized all these people would lose their damn minds, I never would have done it," said the eastern bluebird, adding that there was no way it could preen its feathers in peace when it was being gawked at "like some kind of freak."

Or this one:

Negative Parent-Teacher Conference Not Exactly Eye-Opening For Area Mother

The article tells us:

Andrea Hopkins confirmed on Wednesday that the negative parent-teacher conference she had for her third-grade son, Nate, was not exactly eye-opening. "Oh, so you're saying he's fidgety and doesn't get along well with others? – yeah, not exactly the shocker of the century,"

These excerpts, from The Onion, may make us chuckle, but they epitomize another phrase used in software programming. Tech Target defines this phrase: "a variation on the term garbage in garbage out is 'garbage in, gospel out' and refers to a tendency to put unwarranted faith in the accuracy of computer-generated data."

Contemporary work environments bring unique stresses. Long hours mean we are often working tired and depleted, which may cause mistakes. Employees change jobs more frequently than happened in the past. Companies merge due to buyouts. These factors and many others cause human error. There is a much greater chance that faulty information may have been "put in."

Because of these human errors, we shouldn't trust the data served up solely because it's on the internet. Or more accurately, because it's on a website on the internet. The data needs to be challenged and questioned.

There's no doubt that computers, and even more so now that computers are in our pockets (smartphones), create a sense of *complacency*. We think the world's information is available to us with a swipe. This can lull us into a false sense of security, about the information we are receiving.

But the information may or not be accurate. The best way, for us to move forward in the computer age, is to maintain a sense of skepticism, about the data a computer serves up. We should be asking: Who wrote the data? Is the data verifiable by other sources (challenge the data), and are those sources simply reiterating the data (Rinse repeat phenomena)? Is the site where the data is located the original source of the data, referencing the methods used to create the data, or is the site simply a data meme, as it were?

Perhaps, we need some kind of internet seal, similar to the Good Housekeeping Seal of Approval, for sites that guarantee their information is accurate? What do you think? Email me, as I always enjoy the feedback from readers.

Action Step

Vegan days are a significant change from the way most of us eat. I've had many vegan friends, and been influenced by their eating habits. Taking a vegan day, once each week, pushes us to think a bit longer about the source of the foods we are eating. Taking a vegan day pushes us to think deeper about what pesticides are on our food and where the foods are sourced from. Particularly important for children, whose smaller bodies will be disproportionately affected by pesticides.

Many people think organic foods are more expensive, but this isn't true. In most kitchens, the waste bin is full of thrown-out food; this throwaway food happens much less with organic foods. This could be because we are aware of the cost, or because when we buy organic, we are more aware of the food and choose better ways of cooking, presenting, and eating it.

Even on non-vegan days, the other six days, I try to eat free-range chicken and grass-fed beef. That said, when I'm at a conference and it's inconvenient to find organic food, since I'm doing the best I can for my body most of the time, I go ahead and eat with my conference friends, whatever it is they've chosen to eat. This is a better choice than being obsessive over food.

Of course, as my wife and I have had children, I've become much more aware of the source of food, which is in our home, and which we feed them. We don't deny our children any specific food such as candy or other sweets, but give them very small amounts of foods that we don't think are good for them.

This is the bowl-of-candy-on-the-counter theory. What's denied is what is desired. By letting our children see the candy is there, on the counter, and letting them have small amounts, we don't deny them. The candy does not become a desired treat because it is a denied treat. Makes sense, yeah?

Chapter 14

Can You Quickly

I never took a day off in my twenties. Not one.

Bill Gates, American,
Philanthropist & Co-Founder Microsoft Corporation

We have created a new measurement system with computers and smartphones and our reliance on the world wide web. I call this new time measurement: *the internet second.*

The internet second came about, because of my amazement when calling a business, for a minor situation I needed help with. The customer service representative apologized for the *length of time* it was taking to provide me assistance. Apologizing even though I knew the computer was crunching away pulling up the necessary information the representative needed to solve the problem for me. I, meanwhile, was waiting patiently and thinking nothing of the (actual) small amount of time, less than a couple of minutes, which had gone by.

The world, I concluded later, had moved to an entirely new way of viewing the passage of time. A few *internet seconds* had become too long to wait, and to placate the waiting consumer required social lubrication, with apologies from the representative. This seems a bit nuts.

But, then again, by my best, non-scientific measure, an internet second is about one-tenth the length of a regular second. Thus, an internet hour *equivalent* is now six actual minutes. But who can possibly wait that long?

This change in our perception of time, our use of the internet second, didn't happen overnight. Its intermediary was the microwave and the microwave second. Like Pavlov's dogs, we became conditioned to quickly heating a cup of water for tea in two minutes, rather than waiting for a kettle to heat, and whistle at us that it was ready. This stove top method of heating took *at least twenty minutes*.

Now, in less than an internet second, with a scant swipe, we can find the current temperature, where a movie is playing and at what time, and order a new pair of shoes, delivered by Zappos in a jiffy (free delivery and free returns if they don't fit!).

Software engineers fully grasp the pressures of this instantaneous, *internet second* world. We are living and running our businesses, in this world of *time collapse*. While business is business and life is life, as the saying goes, life and business remain hard. There are always new situations to face and solve; change makes things hard. Ben Horowitz summed this up best, when he called these situations and changes, *hard things*.

"That's the hard thing about hard things – there is no formula for dealing with them," writes Ben Horowitz, author of *The Hard Thing About Hard Things: Building A Business When There Are No Easy Answers*. There is a reason for his book title. Horowitz, and the technology industry, feel the pressure of working against a continuous clock; there is no reprieve from competition on the internet. The competition is *immediate* on the internet.

The Internet Clock

Even when programmers are sleeping, the internet clock is working, tick-tocking away like the crocodile, who swallowed the alarm clock in Peter Pan. The ticking of the clock alerts Captain Hook that the crocodile is near. And looking to eat Captain Hook.

There are crocodiles on the internet hunting for their Captain Hooks. Horowitz, at times, felt like Captain Hook; prey for the internet crocodiles. And he faced some fierce crocodile moments in business, unsure if he would escape becoming his competitor's next meal.

These crocodile moments are the basis of his book. Horowitz is keenly aware that when we are in business, there are innumerable competitors, all around the globe, who aren't sleeping when we sleep. The competitors are seeking out any advantage they can, and they will use any advantage they can without remorse or second thought. While we are snoozing, the competitors would love to eat our breakfast, lunch, dinner, snacks, and pizza.

One of Horowitz's chapters, in the *The Hard Things*, is titled "Peacetime CEO/Wartime CEO." But I'd lop off the first half of that title, and call the chapter, "Wartime CEO." In today's competitive world, it's always wartime, and CEOs are perpetually in "Wartime CEO" mode, at least if they plan on being and staying successful.

Horowitz's current company, without a doubt, shades his perspective. Andreessen Horowitz is a venture capital firm funneling money to startup companies, who seek to create a new product, or to disrupt business as it currently exists, with a competitive product (*the disruptor*).

In the past, a would-be company founder dusted off his hat, shined his shoes, tucked his chin, and trundled over to the local bank. If lucky, he was *given* a business loan by his bank, as long as he put the family house up as collateral, and paid an exorbitant, non-negotiable interest rate on the loan to the bank. For years and years.

Today, most startups, at least technology startups, begin their search for funding with the venture capital firms. One of the primary reasons founders seek out the venture capital firms is the funding comes quickly. VCs, excited by a company, fund it much faster than a bank, knowing that every pizza delivered, may deliver a bit of gossip about their company along with the pizza, into the Silicon Valley ether.

No Lollygagging In Business

Can you quickly are the three, most used words in the software industry; software development is a fast and furious business. Rarely does a software business get the market to themselves, allowing them to lollygag their way to market. Very rarely is a software business the sole creator of a product, which is being created in a category. Competition stalks software companies. Competition, in the software industry, is a wolf constantly nipping at the heels of every software company. It makes *quickly* an essential element, a required element of software companies. This was true for Horowitz and his company.

In his book, Horowitz recounts the several times he was absolutely sure that his software company was out of business. If this happened, if his company went bankrupt, his company would be thrown into the software dustbin, with other failed companies. He would be unable to feed his family and himself.

These near-company-death experiences created a singular mindset for Horowitz. He writes, "By my calculation, I was a peacetime CEO for three days and wartime CEO for eight years." As you can see,

Horowitz barely had a breath as a peacetime CEO; he'd probably lop off the "peacetime" if rewriting the chapter, in agreement with me that the sheer hell-bent-for-leather nature of getting software to market decries anything peaceful about the process.

Similarly, in medicine, quickly is not a choice, but demanded by circumstances. But quickly, in medicine, may lead to mistakes where a life can be lost. Human lives, not bits and bytes, are on the line when medical decisions are being made quickly. Dr. Atul Gawande became concerned over mistakes in medicine that could have been avoided with more decision-making time; the mistakes arose from the doing-everything-at-once necessity of medicine.

This was especially true in the emergency room. The scramble of saving a life, in an emergency, resulted in mistakes, overlooked steps, and contaminations which led to infections.

Dr. Gawande begins his examination, of mistakes in medicine, with the pressured immediacy of treating emergency patients. In his book, *The Checklist Manifesto: How To Get Things Right*, he uses the following example.

A patient appears in the emergency room, and is being treated by a colleague. Initially, the wound doesn't seem horribly bad. The patient has, what seems to be, a knife wound. But as they begin treating the wound, unimaginable amounts of blood began pouring out, flooding the floor.

Soon, with a few very specific questions, they find out that the wound is from a *bayonet*. All the blood, pouring out onto the floor, is because the wound has gone much deeper than the doctors believed it did; they'd been fooled because they'd assumed it was a knife wound.

A bayonet, as the more than half-a-million soldiers, who died during the Civil War would tell us if they could, causes a terrible wound because it goes deep into the body cavity. Because of its length, the attacker doesn't need to be precise to cause significant damage. The sheer reach of the bayonet gives it opportunity to cause harm. A bayonet's push into the body can cut several organs at once. Even if the bayonet only cuts one organ, the deeper the organ, the more likely the blood will pool inside the body, as the emergency room doctors experienced with their patient. This pooling, inside the body, doesn't give the visual signal that the wound is serious and life threatening.

The evaluation by the doctors that it was a knife wound was a false assumption. Hard to fault them. How many of us have even seen a bayonet, or would consider that one might stab us, or has stabbed the patient we are seeing in the ER?

What Else Causes Problems?

Digging deeper, Dr. Gawande evaluated the uniqueness of the time constraints faced by the doctors. He evaluated *time* as a critical component, in the emergency room and in surgery. Once surgery begins, every hour under anesthesia is considered additional risk. A person lying on a surgical table, with their body open, is at great risk. We aren't meant to have our bodies lying open, ever. There are all kinds of germs and bacteria floating around in the air or on the surfaces of the surgical equipment. And no amount of pre-surgical scrubbing or wearing surgical gloves or sterilization of instruments can eradicate them all from the operating room.

He mulls these problems through a philosophical lens. He writes, "The philosophers, Samuel Gorovitz and Alasdair MacIntyre published a short essay on the nature of human fallibility that I read during my surgical training and haven't stopped pondering."

His concern and desire, to care for patients, led him to conclude…as did the writers, Gorovitz and MacIntyre…that two areas were the reason for human fallibility. The first problem area is ignorance; we do not have adequate knowledge to solve the problem. And the second problem area? We are inept; there is knowledge, but we do not apply it correctly.

Dr. Gawande realized little could be done about ignorance. This is conquered through the extended educational inquiry of scholars and, sometimes, by the research of scientists. The research of science was somewhat serendipitous. After all, penicillin, for example, had been a lucky accident when Alexander Fleming left a petri dish with bacteria in it by an open window. Mold had landed on the petri dish and where it landed prevented the bacteria from growing. This discovery spurred Fleming's further inquiry into the nature of mold as an antibiotic.

Dr. Gawande, a well-educated physician, appreciated the educational inquiry of fellow scholars. Nonetheless, he recognized that educational inquiry and scientific research required years or decades, to uncover new solutions for problems. And then, even when the new solutions are proposed, they are studied for years, before becoming accepted scholarship, implemented, and changing the way things are done.

He moved on to what could be controlled.

Ineptness

When confronting the problem of ineptness, Dr. Gawande summarized that we can do better, if we have a structure in place for accessing the knowledge, which will help us. He realized that in the emergency room and in the surgical suite, the cacophony of competing needs combined with time pressures, led to medical steps that were skipped, medical steps inadvertently overlooked, or medical steps wrongly applied, during the treatment. If any of these circumstances occurs, the patient can die.

Can you quickly is an inevitable component of these medical situations. In emergency situations, it's impossible to avoid. But Dr. Gawande realized that many of the failures in medicine, which were occurring, could be averted; they should not *happen*. These are *avoidable failures*.

Dedicated, to finding a solution that would save patient lives, Dr. Gawande identified an engineering concept, referred to as "forcing functions"; situations that demand a distinct set of behavioral responses, each and every time the situation appears. These behavioral responses require nothing more than a preconditioned, reflexive implementation of the predetermined steps.

To ensure that these forced functions take place, he developed a *checklist* for surgeries. The checklist ensured, because it was a brief checklist, that certain steps were taken *at precise times* during the surgery. *Brief* is a key aspect of the checklist. Too long or too complex, and the checklist will be ignored and, hence, be useless.

As an example, the use of antibiotics must be administered during a small window of time, before a surgery begins. Administering the antibiotic early or late, and the antibiotic isn't effective in controlling infection. Patients, after surgery, with uncontrolled infections may die or experience severe complications. The antibiotics save untold numbers of lives every year, but again, they must be given to the patient at exactly the right time.

And you may ask, did his checklist work? Yes, the checklist did work. Dr. Gawande found he has "yet to get through a week of surgery without the checklist leading us to catch something we would have missed."

If you're going to have surgery, you might want to inquire if your medical team uses a checklist. The doctors and nurses may be the smartest people in the room, but even they forget things, miss things. Or they may believe someone else has performed the medical step, such as giving the antibiotic, when in fact it was overlooked. The checklist prevents human error and could save a life, your life or the life of someone you love.

We All Miss Things

With, so many competing *attention demands* each day, it's impossible not to forget something we need to do, we're supposed to do. In an online marketing world, where competition is a click away, we'll lose market share if we aren't the best. The competition seeks to be cheaper and better than the rest of the pack.

In business, we are living on the inside of a perpetual-motion machine of internet marketing that seems to be getting faster. Cheaper, faster, better. These are all wartime signals for businesses; all signs of the competition nipping at our heels. And if the competition is a click away, you can lose everything by being a bit slow out of the gate. This wasn't possible when I started developing games to sell, on my Commodore 64 as a kid, more than thirty years ago. But whether we like it or not, we must acclimate to the world, as it is. And then compete and compete with all we've got. We have to compete with passion and with purpose.

With this in mind, one of the vital core values, at LinkResearchTools, is to work with passion. Our clients depend on us to stay up-to-date and cutting edge. Because of this, my team and I are a tight-knit group.

Together, we are passionate about ensuring that we provide our clients with the best software possible. Every day we are in competition mode.

Passionate Projects

At LRT, it doesn't matter if an employee's passion is for creating graphic design projects, or for working with our clients to assist them in the best use of our software, or for working with the accounting and logistical aspects of managing the company's business, or for ensuring the coding of the software is keeping up with any changes the search engines make to their algorithms. All of these aspects of the business are vital to our success, and as such, I hire and keep people, who have a passion for their jobs. My team reflects my own dedication to making the company successful and to staying committed to providing our clients the best possible support, as they use our software programs.

Having a passion for what you are doing is a guarantee for better results. Grant Cardone is a believer in everyone staying busy and everyone bringing all they've got to work and life. As he says:

White space on your calendar is just room for the devil.

If you have passion for what you do, I guarantee you'll experience joy in your work and you'll take that joy home with you. And you'll have filled in the white space with your goals, and with notes on the action steps needed to achieve those goals. Don't leave room for the devil!

I get up in the morning looking forward to the day because I enjoy my work. I love what I am doing; I love what we are doing as a company. Do you wonder why passion and dedication and joy to the company is important? We spend at least half of our waking time at work, so why be miserable? If you are not passionate about your business, about your job, about your life (and they do all intertwine), then it's time for you to fix whatever needs fixing. For most of us, we don't get a *Groundhog Day*, over and over, as Bill Murray did, to relive the previous day and figure out what we are doing wrong.

Change jobs, change your life. Change something. It will create a domino effect and force you into taking responsibility for where you are in life; if you are miserable, it is your fault and no one else's fault.

The choice is yours and you can do it quickly. You can quit your job and find another one. You can sell all your possessions on eBay, as some have done, and go on that delayed but much desired trip to wherever it is you've been dreaming of going. Don't wait until you've spent your life doing things you don't want to do and are retiring disgruntled, miserable, and in poor health.

And in your job, give all you've got. Learn all you can because you'll take it with you wherever you go. There's no time to lose. Work with passion is our core value. Let it be yours.

Action Step

Checklists work in every area of life in all kinds of ways. A simple checklist task to try is to make a list of five things you'd like to accomplish this week. The tasks can be anything you decide should be on the list.

Clean the closet out? Great. Write it down. Bake cookies with the kids? Put it on the checklist.

Five things should be easy to come up with and you'll be surprised at how great it feels to get to the end of the week and find you've accomplished your list.

In fact, you may find that making lists, and crossing the items off it as they are accomplished, becomes emotionally rewarding. And then you'll decide to make another checklist. And another, until making lists is one of the great habits you've mastered.

Chapter 15

Batch Process

I am writing with my burnt hand about the nature of fire.

Ingeborg Bachmann, Austrian, Poet & Author

Tim Ferris wrote an amazingly successful book, *The 4-Hour Workweek*, on applying *batch processing* to our lives, and *quanted out* a number of ways to achieve this goal. Properly applied, Tim Ferriss pied pipered the idea that your life can be crunched down into various segments, and most of those segments automated, with either outsourcing, or by using a software program, or by deciding to throw out the insignificant aspects of life. Software engineers were way ahead, of Tim, in using batch processing.

Software engineers wouldn't be able to get anything done were it not for batch processing. But batch processing requires diligent, concentrated focus. Once a software engineer becomes immersed in writing code, any distraction or deviation from what they are writing, is a time sink. And scrambling out of the time sink is laborious. Once the mind moves away, from what it was focused on, it must reconnect, find the thread of what it was thinking about, and this is nothing but wasted time. And sometimes, we can never find the thread of thought we were focused on, the indispensable thought we needed most; that thought is lost. But batching can help us to avoid these disturbing experiences, by keeping similar tasks together.

Spaghetti Code

A key to writing code, to not falling into the time sink, is the use of batching. One of the principles, that software engineers employ, is to spend their time on the important aspects of writing software. Then, they use the power of computers, as workhorses for the less important software writing tasks; they batch these parts, which need less human attention or decision making, and then let them be batched and written by the computer. Computer batching is frequently achieved with software scripts or software macros, and sometimes using snippets of code from the software repository.

Macros As Batch

If you are unfamiliar with scripts and macros, let me briefly explain. Macros are a recorded series of steps, which can be automated and repeated, saving enormous amounts of time. One of my favorite macros is batching photographs, which is easily done in Photoshop. I can decide to give a selection of photographs, say ten photographs, a brighter look. This may be needed because they were taken when there were a lot of clouds in the sky making it overcast and dull when the photographs were taken.

I can create a series of steps in Photoshop, automate those steps, and apply the same steps to the photographs. Batching smooths out our time, whether it's a software program we are working with and applying to photographs, or whether we are using a batch process, to make cooking easier. Many cooks, for instance, create and freeze the meals for an entire week, on a single day. This makes them easy to pull out and cook later in the week.

If you've read Ferriss' *The 4-Hour Workweek*, you'll recall the essence and premise of the book, is saving time on necessary, but repetitive parts of our lives. That saved time, Ferris sagely conveys, is available for more interesting stuff, working on new projects and new products...or lying in a hammock deciding whether the cloud floating by is a pig or a cow.

To that end, Ferriss' book is about crunching down to four hours of actual work in a week. This, he argues, is achievable using batching. One of the forms of batching, he uses, is outsourcing as many of your tasks as possible. A good idea for many parts of our lives and our work, but is the four-hour workweek reasonable? Is it even possible for most of us? Did Ferriss ever actually have a four-hour workweek? Maybe. Maybe not.

Batching Fails

Ferriss...and although the book is a fascinating read...includes many aspects of batching completely unusable, by almost everyone. For instance, he states that he hasn't checked his email "more than once a week for the last three years...often not for up to four weeks at a time." Whether this is still true, several years after publication of *The 4-Hour Workweek,* is questionable. But there are very few of us, whether in business or in our lives, who could ignore emails for an entire week. Or even an entire day.

This is especially true in an era of computer breaches and the accompanying information thefts, email notifications from our home security systems, and with our kids living far away from us. What mom or dad doesn't check their email daily to see if there is news from their child away at college? What mom or dad isn't checking their email for alerts from their child's school or daycare? Email is critical to our lives, and not to be ignored.

Ferris does advise using a range of *batching timelines* and seeing what works or doesn't work. He advises that he found so few problems with ignoring his emails and other batched tasks that he implemented an even less frequent schedule for batching. He decided to do fewer batches, but more tasks at one time.

This might have worked well for a single bachelor, such as Ferriss, who has no children and no full-time employees, but may not work so well for anyone who isn't a single bachelor, who has children, and who has employees, or whose livelihood depends on an employer. This isn't to say the idea is not valuable, but rather my suggestion is to not use Ferriss' advice directly, but to mold and adapt his ideas to your own life, work, and needs. The theory is a good one, let's agree, if modifications for each person's life and work is included in the process.

Fight The Interruption Impulse

Ferriss very adroitly highlights, what he calls, the *interruption impulse*. This is a larger topic than can be covered here, as it's hard to separate out whether this impulse is a cultural one or a biological one. After all, maybe we are biologically programmed to periodically look around, at preset intervals? Perhaps any focus, for too long, would mean we were *dinne*r?

In early humans, this might have been a way to protect ourselves from predators. If we forgot to look around periodically, perhaps this would give a predator a chance to sneak up on us and attack. Or maybe this interruption impulse is an important culturally-conditioned impulse? Maybe we are wired to reconnect with our fellow humans frequently, as a kind of hive mentality? Robert Putnam, in his book, *Bowling Alone*, explores the importance of social connections, and finds them vital for personal and cultural health. So, although the answers aren't clear, it does seem that interruptions can be very important. They aren't all bad.

For instance, there are howling laments from many corners of the media, about those addicted to checking their smartphones and their emails. The media decries those, who are conditioned to respond instantly to a ping of a text message, regardless of their situation.

These howls have grown quite loud. News reports document the obvious problem of people on their smartphones walking into telephone poles or narrowly avoiding a car, because the person doesn't lift their eyes from the smartphone. Advertisers have had a field day with this topic, by showing parents at the dinner table, engrossed in their smartphones and ignoring their children's tales of their day at school.

But less obvious effects may be more long ranging and worrisome.

What will the result of this constant interruption to our thought process be, as technology ping us? Is technology ruining our ability to have extended period of introspective and concentrated thought? At this time, we don't have the answers. And by the time we do have the answers, it may be too late? We could be short circuiting our neuronal capacity and passing it along genetically? Hopefully, scientists will find out before any real damage is done to our ability to think long and complex thoughts.

However, there are many studies, indicating that an ability to focus is essential to working on and finishing any task. But a concentrated focus is even more essential for the tasks, which require abstract thinking and decision making. The kind of thinking that creatives, like software engineers, require to write software programs.

Software engineers experience this concentrated thinking, as a form of *flow*. The idea of flow has been explored extensively, by Mihaly Csikszentmihalyi (pronounced as Me-High Chick-Sent-Me-High), a

Hungarian psychologist, who has written on the topic in his many books. In *Finding Flow: The Psychology of Optimal Experience*, he writes that "every culture develops *time protective devices* – religions, philosophies, arts, and comforts – that protect us from chaos."

Interviewed, on *Wired*, Csikszentmihalyi said, "Being completely involved in an activity for its own sake. The ego falls away. Time flies. Every action, movement, and thought follows inevitably from the previous one, like playing jazz. Your whole being is involved, and you're using your skills to the utmost."

In order to batch, and get done what needs to be done, one word is applicable. *Now*.

Distractions As Destruction

At work, impulse interruptions are *concept distractions*. When a software engineer is in the middle of writing some code, a distraction is an enormous time cost. He'll lose his train of thought, and find it hard to regain. He'll, possibly, spend hours figuring out how to pick up the thread of his thinking. Where was I? he'll wonder. In business, we can't afford to lose all this time. Cumulatively, over a few weeks or a few months, how many hours are spent trying to recover the complex thoughts, of where we were on the project?

Unfortunately, we build these impulse interruptions into our lives, and become habituated to them, whether we admit it or don't admit it. The interruptions begin in the morning, when we start poking around the computer, reading through dozens of emails; we have Facebook open and are getting notifications from our friends; we decide to send out a tweet on Twitter; we remember something is in our Amazon cart, and click over to Amazon because we've decided to go ahead and pay for the items. Get the order on its way to us.

These distractions are a bare few of the many that start in the morning, and then intrude into the rest of the day. If we let them, distractions can gobble up the entire day, without mercy. Programmers are all too familiar with this distraction problem.

When a software engineer, or anyone deeply involved in a project is focused, once they are removed from that focus because of an interruption, much is lost. We cannot return to a blinking cursor in our mind; a mind is very different from a computer. The thoughts that were connected, once disconnected, are lost. Sure, maybe there are remnants. But, usually, there is the *what was I thinking*? We root around in the neurons, trying to find that crucial thought, the one that was moving us forward, but which is lost.

To combat these concept distractions, these impulse interruptions, at LinkResearchTools, we have workplace guidelines and techniques that allow everyone to achieve flow. And to stay focused. One of our guidelines is based on an easy visual prompt. If we see someone with their headset on, we do not speak with them. We see, by the visual prompt, they may be speaking with a client of our company, and it's essential to not interrupt them.

We, also, have a technique of communication using the Slack program. With Slack, we maintain real-time messages that can be opened, checked to find any needed information, or ignored, as suits the employee. Thus, as the work pace of the employees allows, they can check to see if new information is available, or not check it all day, depending on how focused on their project they are, at that time. We've found that

Slack provides for a sense of autonomy for employees, something that reinforces a self-motivation ethic.

A certain number of life events, at work and home, simply must be taken care of whether you want to or don't want to. This is a contraindication, which contrasts with many of the messages served up by the entertainment industry. Speakers, books, and movies, entreat us to "live today." Some, of the so-called gurus, preach you should live every day, as though it is your last. But really? Doesn't that sound pretty stupid?

Only Today Matters?

This is ridiculous. If you thought today was your last day alive, you wouldn't bother to: renew your driver's license, wash your clothes, or skip dessert, so you can hit the goal of losing ten pounds.

However, if you are reading this, there is a good chance you will be here tomorrow, and the day after tomorrow, and the day after tomorrow. Thus, a better way to live is to *batch what you can*; batch the repetitive, non-rewarding parts. Choose Tim Ferriss' method and outsource these repetitious tasks. Between batching and outsourcing, you reserve most of your time for the activities and experiences that bring you the joy, fun, and freedom.

One aspect of business is considered as unworthy of our time. Tim Ferriss and Jeff Bezos agree that meetings are an unproductive aspect of work. Meetings should be avoided if possible, and if that isn't possible, the meeting should be kept to a small group. Bezos applies a two-pizza rule; he believes that the number of people attending a meeting should not exceed the number, which can be fed by two pizzas. Ferriss goes further and suggests avoiding meetings altogether.

Ferriss explains the use of a *Puppy Dog Close* to avoid meetings. He explains it like this:

I'd like to go to the meeting, but I have a better idea. Let's never have another one, since all we do is waste time and not decide anything useful.

What is Ferriss thinking?

Alright. It is necessary to have meetings. We need to exchange ideas and share information; this is what humans do and have always done. After all, you could technically call huddling around a fire in a cave, chomping on a hunk of meat and pinging each other, so to speak, about where to run the herd off a cliff so those waiting at the bottom of the cliff can collect their meat and hides, a meeting.

Those cave meetings, leading to the hunt, must have been popular, as scientists have found numerous sites, which indicate this kind of hunting by humans.

Some of these sites are even UNESCO designated World Heritage Sites, such as this one in Canada, the Head-Smashed-In Buffalo Jump World Heritage Site:

The Jump bears witness to a method of hunting practiced by native people of the North American plains for nearly 6,000 years. This archaeological site, known around the world, preserves the remarkable history of the Plains People through the millennia. Because of their excellent understanding of the regional topography and bison behavior, the native people were able to hunt bison by stampeding them over a cliff. They then carved up the carcasses and dragged the pieces to be butchered and processed in the butchering camp set up on the flats beyond the cliffs.

Meetings, as you see, can lead to a productive result. We can't avoid them, but we can make them lead to a desired end.

A Busy World

As Tim Ferriss expands on the topic of batching, he uses the example of a business saving money by printing multiple t-shirts at once, rather than printing them one at a time. He recognizes that batching is not a new way of doing things or his original idea, referencing *The Cost of Not Paying Attention: How Interruptions Impact Knowledge Worker Productivity*, by Jonathan B. Spira and Joshua B. Feintuch.

In fact, productivity is, arguably, the single greatest topic of our time. Feeling time crunched, we are all looking for a new and better advantage that will allow us to be more productive. The productivity problem, and the search for solutions to the problem, is one of the primary reasons that Ferriss' book was propelled to its place on best seller lists.

Using as many shortcuts, as we can, is vital. Being efficient results in each of us using our time to give ourselves more of what we want, and lessen those elements of work and life we don't want to waste our time on. I'd much rather spend the afternoon playing with my children, listening to their laughter, than crunching software.

But there is an alternative problem once we have all that free time. We need to fill our days, something most of us have never had to think about. Most of us have been subject to our employer's schedule, or our school schedule, or our parent's schedule. Free time, lots of it, is not a situation most people have encountered in their lives.

I mean, let me ask you, if you could manage to run your whole business in four hours a week, as Ferriss has said he did, what would you do with all the rest of your time? Party the rest of the 164 hours in that week? (There are 168 hours in a week, if you do the easy multiplication of 24 hours times the 7 days making up a week, and subtract your 4 working hours, you'll find you have 164 *play hours*.)

So, after the four hours you work, you're left with 164 hours. You must then decide what you'll fill them with? Would you play basketball or ride your bike all day? Watch movies? Volunteer? Or hang out with your family?

Chances are you'd get bored quickly with sports and chances are your family would be busy doing other things. After all, they haven't figured out how to run their lives in four hours a week, and they'd soon be annoyed that you are in their way, because unless they've figured out how to work four hours a week, they've still an awful lot to do each day.

As odd as it may seem, when there are ceaseless complaints about going to work from those people around us, there are many rich people, who work even as they enter their "mature" years. Warren Buffett is approaching ninety, and continues to work at his company, Berkshire Hathaway, Inc. Rupert Murdoch is close to ninety, and still heads up his company, 21st Century Fox, although his sons have taken over many of his duties. Mick Jagger is in his mid-seventies, and performing concerts with The Rolling Stones. Jagger had his eighth child, in 2017. (In case you're wondering, Jagger has four boys and four girls.) Elizabeth II, Queen of the United Kingdom, Canada, Australia, and New Zealand, is in her nineties, and working for her people, by maintaining a monthly calendar of appearances.

Maybe work is something *you want to do*, if you take pride in your work and find it rewarding?

A friend of mine spoke with Tim Ferriss, and as I understand their conversation, Ferriss realizes that most people won't be able to reduce their work life to four hours a week. Rather, the goal is reducing your routine dull tasks, editing out your boring tasks. This is an excellent idea, because if we track our time for a week, most of us will find that many of our day's hours are not used wisely or in an efficient manner. Thus, Ferriss' suggestion, of a 4-hour workweek, is more of a life prompt; he wants you to focus on those areas that can be redesigned, edited out, reduced down, or outsourced. This lets you spend your free time for the beneficial and rewarding aspects of life.

For instance, if you spend four hours a week on annoying stuff, like paying bills and invoices and taxes, that's acceptable. But if you are spending twenty hours a week, doing these boring tasks, by default your time and energy for the money-making tasks, the career advancement tasks, or the life-enjoying hours, will be limited. This is wasting your life. You are draining your energy with the tasks that don't add to the bottom line, improve your career, or bring happiness into your life. This is what *The 4-Hour Workweek* is all about.

It is true that life can, at times, be repetitive and it can be tedious. That said, we aren't washing clothes with a wringer washer, as our grandmothers did, and then hanging the clothes out to dry on the clothesline, waiting for them to dry, and then folding them, bringing them into the house, and ironing the ones that need ironing. That was truly repetitive and tedious. Today, much of our life's work is automated. We have an endless array of time-and-labor saving devices.

And what of Tim Ferriss? How much of his work is he batching? He seems to be a pretty busy guy, writing books, creating podcasts, being interviewed. Maybe the Redditors (Reddit has a vocal and enthusiastic group of posting enthusiasts.) should ask him?

Of course, the point is that not everything works for everyone. Ferriss made this point succinctly, even as he pushed us all to think differently, and to act differently, in performing the activities of work and life. And the fundamental principle, to consider how we can be more efficient, effectively buying more time for our lives and work, is one of the great principles we can, and should, live by. Our kids, our spouses, our employers, and our employees, will all benefit when we free ourselves from unnecessary, mundane tasks.

Action Step

I've noted previously, but it's a relevant point, so I'll note it again. We need to spend time periodically evaluating our life. And sometimes, another person can give us the best perspective. Ask your friends or family or your employees or coworkers, what aspects of your life they see that could be batched. Take notes and spend some "alone time" giving consideration to their answers. Even if you don't agree with them, I promise, you'll be very surprised by their answers.

Do they think you are wasting time on things you shouldn't?

Chapter 16

Big Data

I had a dream last night that a hamburger was eating me.

Jerry Seinfeld, American, Actor

Two words that give marketers and advertisers heart palpitations, in a good way, are the words *big data*. Big data, succinctly, is the collection of everything about you that can be collected as data, and turned into information to sell you services and products.

You *are* the target of the algorithm crunching that runs the internet and creates big data. More specifically, your wallet is the target. The goal of marketers and advertisers is creating a profile on you. The better they profile you, the more specifically you can be shown advertising, and that advertising result in your purchasing their services and products.

In other words, search engines are not your friend. Oh, sure, they try to look friendly. Google, for instance, has those cute, friendly-looking cartoons, called "doodles," on their homepage. At Halloween, the doodle is a witch sitting on a broom sweeping across the sky. At Easter, they have a little bunny rabbit doodle, in the pastel colors of spring, carrying lots of chocolate eggs in an Easter basket. For most of the significant, recognized events and celebrated holidays of the year, Google's *doodlers* create a new doodle. They sometimes celebrate an eminent person, on the homepage, with a doodle. Very warm and fuzzy.

But Google doesn't have the incredible number of software engineers they do (rough estimate places this at 20,000 software engineers), so they can bring a smile to your face. Let's take a look at what Google really is and does.

Google's Search Presents Advertising

Google, according to Alexa (Alexa is owned by Amazon. Alexa tracks visits to websites and uses that information to rank websites.), is the top visited website on the internet. The second most visited website, according to Alexa, is YouTube, which is owned by Google. According to SearchEngineLand:

> *Recent information, released by Google, has shown that more and more users are using YouTube as a search engine. Searches related to "how to" on YouTube are growing 70% year over year. It is no secret that video content is more engaging than a page of text and can be much more informative. YouTube's popularity and reach are expanded by its inclusion in both Google Web and Video search.*

The article further explains, "Google weeded out the video competition in web search by predominantly displaying video-rich snippets for YouTube videos back in 2014."

Hmmm. So, Google, the de facto leading search engine, *finds* that its own company, YouTube, has the best "video rich snippets." A bit self-serving?

And are you aware that when you search, on a search engine like Google or Bing or Yahoo, there are two different results, which you see? There are the *paid* results and the *organic* results?

The paid results are those results that companies pay the search engine advertising dollars for. This places their advertisements directly in front of you. This paid advertising is how Google makes the massive amounts of money piling up in its coffers. There is, of course, absolutely nothing wrong with paying for advertising. Or for being the company, which makes its revenue by providing advertising, such as Google and Bing and Yahoo, or any other search engine, does. Without advertising, we wouldn't be aware of the many products that we might be interested in. Advertising makes us aware of these, possibly, useful products.

However, there are, also, the organic results that search engines show in the search results. These are the naturally occurring results. The algorithm believes these results are what seek and need for your purpose, whether you are searching for information or to purchase a product. These are the so-called *free* results. The free results may, or may not, be your best result. It may be that the advertised results will have what you need most, and that they are your best result. It's a very complex situation with many varying factors to consider.

The Best Results

We need to remember that the results, which show up when we search, are a result of very complex algorithms that are constantly changing. These algorithms, and the factors they use to determine what you want, are too complex to explain here, but suffice to say that the search engines are striking bargains with the devil. After all, if you are backlinked from great sites, because you have an authentic, well-loved and valued website, your company can get tremendous amounts of traffic, tremendous numbers of customers, coming to your site without paying a search engine a single cent. This is not advantageous for a search engine's bottom line. And whether it is Google or Bing or Yahoo or another search engine, each of them wants as much of a company's money, from advertising, as it can possibly obtain. Absolutely nothing wrong with that goal.

Ultimately, though, this is all about *the data*. Or rather the collected and profiled data, as it relates to a search engine's advertising products. Google's big data and Google's advertising products are so entwined, they are virtually inseparable. The same is true for Yahoo and Bing and the other search engines.

At its heart, search engines are the ultimate in big data collection and crunching. Unbelievably big data. If a search engine believes it can collect and store the number of breaths you take per minute, it will. If a search engine believes it can collect data, on whether you are the kind of person, who will stop on the street and pick up a penny, it will.

Google Needs The Money

Why, you might ask, does a search engine, like Google, need so much money from advertisers?

How else could it make the money to pay the, more than, 60,000 employees that currently work there? (Interesting point: As noted previously, Google has around 20,000 software engineers. Thus, with around 60,000 total employees, this indicates that one in three Google employees is a software engineer.) And how could it afford to give them all their free stuff? Googlers get free gourmet meals, on-site games to play like billiards, volleyball, and ping pong, as well as free haircuts. Nap pods are available for an employee, who wants to take a quick snooze. (Nap pods?!) And it isn't just Google, of course. The large tech companies are incredibly generous in their benefits and perks for employees.

So even with giving away all that stuff, Google's parent company, Alphabet, is said to be worth almost 700 billion dollars. Microsoft, according to Fortune, is worth 507 billion dollars. Wouldn't you love to see the numbers, on how many advertisements, Google and Microsoft (Bing) show to consumers every day to make that much money? (And yes, these companies have other aspects of their business bringing in considerable amounts of revenue.)

Nonetheless, Google, Bing, and Yahoo, exist because they are *advertisement selling companies*. The biggest advertisement selling companies in the world. All the search engines, big and small, are advertising companies.

Who Doesn't Love Free?

Google, Bing, Yahoo, and the other search engines, like all advertising companies, realize people love free stuff. Free is the single greatest advertising word. Always has been, and may always be. So, besides giving free stuff to their employees, Google, as an example, will give *you free stuff*, with one condition. In return, you do have to let them collect data, and based on that data, show you lots and lots of their advertising.

To entice you, and gain more information about you, yes, Google gives you free email, free analytics for businesses, free office support software, such as Google docs and their free spreadsheet program. These free office software programs have yet to be a Microsoft Office killer, but for those without professional demands or who are on a budget, they work pretty well. If you choose, Google will happily bump you up to their full programs, the Google Suite, but you do pay for these bulked-up, complete programs. They are, as Google says, *"Chosen by millions of businesses, from small companies to the Fortune 500."*

185

But the algorithms are clicking away, or rather *logging your clicking away*: they know who you are, where you are, and what you like. Every click you make sends them more information about you. In addition, some of their collected data about you comes from your use of their free software programs (as noted above). According to Wikipedia:

> *Google has been criticized for its practice of automatically scanning documents for keywords that violate the terms of service, and censoring those documents.*

This system that Google uses, is incredibly effective. They mash the collected, big data information about you into their algorithms, and match that with their advertisers focus, to show you ads that will entice you to purchase. After all, if Google can't properly target ads, so that you see *and buy*, what the advertisers pay them to place in front of you, the advertisers will stop paying them. Maybe another search engine will do a better job?

At that point, the Reign of Google, as the most used of the search engines, is over. Google doesn't want this to happen. This isn't discussed much. Most of the articles about Google, found across the internet, proclaim how wonderful Google is as a search engine. This completely misrepresents what Google is. Again, Google is *an advertising company*, and any other categorization misrepresents them, is a form of bit-and-byte, snake-oil, elixir salesmanship. That's my opinion.

All this free stuff means we are *users* of Google, and note that again… *users not customers*…since those of us using the Google-it search engine, don't pay a dime for all the free stuff.

Supposedly, with your free access to the search engines, and in response to your query, you are receiving the best, most accurate, results on the internet, in response to your search. Hmm. Maybe and maybe not. Skeptics have been calling the search engine results, and their overt manipulation by them, not really the *best* search engine results for your query, but rather, the best results for you that *coordinate with what an advertiser* wants to sell you.

Google and Microsoft, rather Microsoft's search engine, Bing, have said they no longer (purportedly) collect information about you from your use of their programs, when you are writing or creating or saving or sending stuff with the software programs. But what is being scanned into Google's or Microsoft's giant, vast search algorithms? Are we to believe that there is no leakage, from our use of the programs, into their giant databases? And is there any kind of second-party verification that this is the case? With companies as large as Google and Microsoft are, who can possibly monitor them for abusive practices?

It's impossible to know, because Google and Microsoft and the other search engines don't say *exactly* how all those thoughts and writings of yours, with their various programs, are being used and manipulated by the algorithms. Or how those thoughts and writings of yours are logged into some giant, forever, all-about-you-information-database, which in some weird way that they can later disclaim that "they weren't aware of," was working with their advertising programs. Various methods of "spying" on consumers crops up in the news consistently; the media reports another *revelation* that a company has "inadvertently" monitored activity, which its privacy policy declaims it doesn't monitor.

They Know Who You Are

According to mid-2017 press releases, and as quoted from a NY Times article, Google will no longer scan emails:

Google plans to abandon its longstanding practice of scanning user email in its Gmail service to serve targeted advertising...the service has been criticized by privacy advocates for scanning email to generate contextually aware ads. The ads, in emails, bothered users more than other targeted advertising found across the web, because users are more touchy about the privacy of email versus, for example, browsing history.

Similarly, Microsoft has made statements emphasizing their dedication to consumer privacy. They have attempted to assuage the worries of consumers, who are their privacy is being invaded when using Microsoft's services. At PCWorld, there is an extensive article on this topic, which states in part:

Microsoft made it clear that, at least for advertising purposes, it does not listen in on your private communications. "As part of our ongoing commitment to respecting your privacy, we have updated the Microsoft Services Agreement to state that we do not use what you say in email, chat, video calls, or voicemail to target advertising to you," the company said. "Nor do we use your documents, photos, or other personal files to target advertising to you."

Google and Microsoft are, of course, not Mother Teresa. And they make no claim to sainthood.

Still.

Bordering on a monopoly, Google was fined with a giant penalty from the European Union in 2017. And how about the EU, the European Union, even identifying Google as being involved in antitrust activities?

The EU said Google abuses its power, pushes down search results of competitive products from other price comparison engines like

NexTag, PriceGrabber, and Yahoo. The EU determined that Google's overwhelming presence, in the market, was so large that the other search engines simply couldn't compete.

This has been an ongoing problem, and will continue to be a long term and difficult problem. The EU decision addresses issues that have been going on since 2008. They finally came to a decision and penalized Google with a 2.7 billion dollar (€2.4 billion) fine.

But the real question is, will Google continue this practice? Is a 2.7 billion fine an obstacle or impediment to Google's way of doing business?

As currently estimated, Google earned more than 90 billion dollars in 2016; this makes the fine a small amount of money for Google. Businesses have long been willing to suffer some fines, even large ones, if they make enough money to justify them. Imagine that Google decides to up the cost of every advertisement by a penny? How many fines from the EU would that additional revenue pay?

The long-term question, though, is how often the EU will run through the machinations of an antitrust determination, fine Google for its (purported) antitrust acts, and repeat this same process, again and again? It seems futile unless a bigger, stronger stick can be found.

And lest we forget…Google, rather than paying the fine to the EU, can hire as many lawyers as they want, swamp the EU with paperwork demanding "information" and "clarification." Google can decide to dance the dance of litigation "to infinity and beyond.…"

In that case, will the EU spend the same money fighting back? Not likely. Google will delay, litigate the fine and the decision, and continue running their business as usual. Good luck, European Union!

And as Google, and not to be *discriminatory*, other search engines such as Firefox, Yahoo, Bing, Baidu, and AOL, provide you results, they continue to create even more giant databases about you, your family, your friends, and associates. Of course, it's not just the search engines. Many websites are using very sophisticated tracking programs to determine, who is visiting their websites. Even if you don't fill out any forms on the website, or order anything, there are programs that can determine who has been visiting the website.

And all this information is the ultimate in big data.

In her fascinating and awe-inspiring book, *Weapons of Math Destruction: How Big Data Increases Inequality and Threatens Democracy,* highly-acclaimed author, Cathy O'Neil, explores the benefits and the costs of big data. Here is an elegant and simple summation of the thesis of her book:

> *We live in the age of the algorithm. Increasingly, the decisions that affect our lives – where we go to school, whether we get a car loan, how much we pay for health insurance – are being made not by humans, but by mathematical models. In theory, this should lead to greater fairness...but the opposite is true. The models being used today are opaque, unregulated, and uncontestable, even when they're wrong. More troubling, they reinforce discrimination.*

O'Neil provides some frightening examples. Here's one from her book.

A young man, who'd encountered some mental health problems (relatively minor), and been treated, finds himself unable to be hired at even a menial, low-wage job. Even though he was a stellar college student. The information from years before is haunting him, even though he took the steps to seek help. The data is following him wherever he goes and is preventing him from his potential success.

Of course, according to the daticians and the statisticians, all this data could, would, and should, be used to the advantage of people and companies. Not to continue to hurt them, after a situation has been corrected.

O'Neil addresses this advantage in her book. The "strategically vital job for HR departments is to locate future stars, the people whose intelligence, inventiveness, and drive, can change the course of an entire enterprise," says O'Neil. This could make big data incredibly advantageous if it is used in this way.

Or maybe big data could be used advantageously to change the course of history?

Algorithms Have Many Benefits

When watching the movie, *The Big Short: Inside The Doomsday Machine*, it was fascinating to see the portrayals of some of the really smart people, who work in the financial industry. Michael Burry is a hedge fund manager, as portrayed by Brad Pitt, in the movie. He says that he was not duplicitous enough to date well or interact with others well. (The ability to lie well, as a dating asset could, no doubt, fill several, very lengthy books.)

He recounts that he posted a bare-the-truth profile of himself on a dating website, in order to meet a woman. And his future wife responded to it. She, he says, wanted someone, who was honest in their profile.

As this example shows, algorithms certainly have positive aspects we can consider when making decisions. They give us can statistics and data that can improve our decisions, change our course of action. The movie is grounded in the fact that the data, from financial algorithms, changed Burry's investing course of action. But the algorithms are not human, and they don't allow for human introspection and understanding.

For instance, if Burry been applying for a job with a company, would a hiring algorithm have seen his abilities? Maybe the algorithm would have wanted to hire a truly honest employee, an amazingly talented guy, and found his blunt honesty a valuable personality trait? Or maybe it would have found Burry an odd guy, and treated him like the example of the young man in O'Neil's book, the guy who was denied a job because of his past mild, mental health difficulties?

These algorithms, though, are irrelevant if they are not used to our benefit. In the movie, *The Big Short*, there is a very harsh examination of the blatant, cover-our-eyes-and-pretend-we-don't-see-it, ignoring of those machinations taking place in the financial markets that led to the 2008 collapse. Of course, as the movie makes the point, Burry… and a few others…did notice. And as with Enron, a lot of people had to *deny* they saw the problems, or they would be morally complicit in the pain that accompanies the ruination of the finances and lives that follow these collapses. There were many people, who knew the 2008 crash was coming.

Burry was one of those, who saw and believed what the algorithms predicted; he told many others and some of those he told were in the financial industry, but he was ignored. He was a Paul Revere galloping his horse, swinging his lantern, and warning of the forthcoming crash.

This was an advantage of the algorithms; the information was evident and could have stymied the devastating effects of the 2008 financial crash, had more people paid attention, rather than ignoring the imminent weapons of math destruction. As it turned out, Burry made a fortune for himself and his investors by seeing what was there to be seen, and capitalizing on it, when the crash occurred.

Other financial experts, who were warning of the problems in the market, were ignored, as Burry was ignored. But maybe it didn't matter. It could be we were too far down the path of financial ruin. The crash simply had to happen. But, perhaps, the crash could have been lessened, at least somewhat, if the early warnings had been heeded and taken note of.

We can't change history. 2008 is in the past. But we can debate fiercely, and we should debate fiercely, how the software that software engineers are writing should, would, and can, be used. To this end, software programmers are engaged in debates, on the various moral points, of the software we write.

We sit around with a beer in hand discussing the merits of our programs and how we *are* responsible for the results that derive from them. We are very aware that these results change behavior, can move the culture to a new way of thinking, and can even bring down political regimes. The Arab Spring is an excellent example, of the powerful of software programs, in creating change.

The A & The B of Software

Software engineers sometimes use, what is called, A/B testing of the software programs. This means that the software engineer creates two versions of a software program and from these two versions, depending on what the desired results are, chooses to use one version of the program rather than the other version. This choice is based on the software engineer's decision regarding which is the *better* result. Of course, *better* is a relative, and very subjective, term based on the software engineer's interpretation of what *better* is. Or, if the software engineer works for someone, the decision of which program is better, A or B, will be their boss's decision.

What does A/B testing mean? It means everything we see or read, on the internet, has self-interested motivation involved in its creation. Every article we read, every website we visit, has an underlying ethos of self-interest, as its reason for existing.

Software engineers understand this well. Ultimately, we are, as with all humans, motivated by self-interest. But we are, also, aware that *we will live with what we code*. We recognize that our families and our friends and our associates will live with what we code. We are, ultimately, guided by what is good for all of us. White hats prevail, which is why there is continuous and lively, sometimes expletive-filled conversations taking place in the world of software engineers, about what the morals of our jobs are.

Action Step One

Rotate your search engines for a week and see how you feel about the results. Did you notice a difference in your search results? Do some of the results seem like they are designed to target certain kinds of advertisements to you, rather than giving you the answers or search results, which will assist you best?

We don't eat pizza, *vitamin P*, for every meal (even software engineers vary their diet!). Why have we become so complacent about using Google for so many searches? After all, it is not the *only* search engine; maybe we are simply in the habit of using it?

Action Step Two

Your friends, associates, and family, may not be conscious of how much information is being collected about them, by their use of the search engines, or that information is being collected when they visit websites. None of us can possibly be aware of how much information is being collected about us, but every keystroke we make is a potential piece of information or data point logged somewhere.

We did, not that many years ago, live without all these electronic devices. Every month, for an entire day, try leaving the computer off, turn off your cell phone. Walk the dog or walk with your spouse. Or your kids.

Wow. So quiet. Do you find yourself talking to each other? Did you forget what quiet sounds like? Hmm…

Chapter 17
Wookies, Coders, and Our AI Masters

When you have made as many mistakes as I have, then you can be as good as me.

Wolfgang Puck,
Austrian, Chef & Restaurateur

The future of coding will, in all likelihood, be written by software engineers with an entirely new programming language. Software programs, and software code, grows old and may lack the functionality needed, as the demands of technology and the internet improve and increase.

Python, for instance, is a powerful software program. Python has been used to write many of the biggest websites on the internet. Released in 1991, almost thirty years ago, Python is the software that was used to create Dropbox, Survey Monkey, Quora. And, oh yeah, it powers Google, which was coded in 1996. But will Python be used in the future?

Software programs that are yet to be created, or even thought up by imaginative men and women, will be required to do things we haven't even considered yet. As the internet expands, and as the one-half of the world that currently is without internet access is brought online, stronger, more robust software programs will be needed and demanded.

This means that we need to consider what we want from technology and the internet, as it builds out. There are a lot of questions to be asked and answered. What do you think the crucial questions will be? Will they be about safety and protecting financial information during transactions? Personal privacy? Privacy for children? Access for all on an equitable level? Should internet access be considered a basic human right in a technological age?

When I ask people those question, while walking through my days, the answers are highly-varied. And no matter what continent I'm on or who I ask, I'm always amazed at how much thought and conversation is going on about how technology will affect us.

No one on the planet, it seems, is unaware of the effect software and technology is having on their lives. Men and women, of all ages and from all walks of life, are being greatly affected by the software that engineers around the globe are writing. Even those among us, who could be considered *computer illiterate*, are aware of the many changes affecting us, because of computers. Everyone seems to be aware that the future will bring changes, but they are changes we can't imagine.

There does seem to be, common knowledge, that when a search engine serves up an ad for a new winter coat directly after you've been looking at the upcoming fall weather report, that the search engine has bounced a *beam cookie* (more formally a tracking packet) that's logged your interest in fall weather, referenced it into a giant database, and then correlated this information to the ad base supporting the search engine's very lucrative advertising business.

After all, Google, Yahoo, and Bing, and other search engines, as I've written, aren't really search engines. They are the largest advertising and data collection businesses ever created in the history of the world. The biggest question of the 21st century is how much data about us we are comfortable with these data collection systems collecting? It's time for ongoing public conversations about technology and how it affects us. Currently, these discussions seem very scattered and irregular.

This is particularly important since, as I noted in an earlier section of this book, the internet is – according to the scientists – twenty percent developed. With our conversations, we can have a lot of influence on how the internet and big data interacts with our lives. We can establish standards before the problems are created, by determining how much intrusion into our private lives, is too much intrusion.

Software Engineers Needed

A lot of software engineers will be needed in the future. In fact, a lot of software engineers will be needed by many companies to assist you in fending off the search engine's decisions about what you should and should not see, by providing you alternative information from a wider decision platform. And to ensure there is lots of competition providing you data. Competition keeps the data honest. To that end, the skills and talents of women, as well as men, needs to be utilized, as fully as possible.

Extensive, ongoing, scientific studies are underway to determine the differences in brain power between men and women. Do the studies, which show women are more verbal and emotional and right-brained, hold water? Do the studies, which show men are more dispassionate and analytical and left-brained, hold water? We won't have answers from these studies for years, and probably, for decades.

But imagine the scientists find that the long-held, preconceived notions (women are more verbal; men are more analytical) are true. What consideration should we give various *natural* talents in hiring software engineers?

Ultimately, in my mind, it's rather irrelevant and a waste of time to spend even a moment on this concern, or give it any weight in our hiring. Unless and until, it is directly shown and can be proven, that certain people have certain skills based on genetics, and that those skills are specifically applicable to a career in software engineering, it's irrelevant to debate that certain characteristics belong primarily to males or to females. And, if and when, the geneticists give us proof that specific skills *are* directly correlated to genetics, we can have an extended conversation on the legalities of hiring based on genetic predispositions or talents. For now, what is relevant is bringing all the skills and talent that can be drawn, *from the human race,* to our needs.

Early Introduction

We give little merit or credit to the development of skills, which are encouraged and enhanced, with early educational experiences.

Bill Gates had access to computer time, at his private school, fifty years ago. Pierre Omidyar, the founder of Paypal, began his interest with software and computers in ninth grade, at his school in Virginia. Mark Zuckerberg, the founder of Facebook, was given tremendous support in learning software, while young. According to Wikipedia, "His father taught him Atari BASIC Programming in the 1990s, and later hired software developer David Newman to tutor him privately."

Early computer use seems to have been (in the past) almost exclusively a male activity. This could have been due to a variety of factors. There were few women, who had dads teaching them about computers thirty years ago? At least, there are few, who've told me they had dads teaching them about computers.

And I've yet to hear anyone consider why, at a private school such as Gates attended, there weren't an equal number of women interested in using computer time? Maybe there were women using computer time and they didn't continue the interest? Maybe the school didn't encourage women, who showed talent for engineering and computers?

Regardless of the standards fifty years ago, computer skills and computer language courses are becoming embedded in the education system for all students. These classes are routinely offered, as course curriculum, and are designed to start students' technology education, as early as possible. Times have clearly changed. Early learning programs are emphasizing STEM programs (Science, Technology and Math), and are designed to keep boys *and girls* in the technology programs. These programs provide support for the development of a foundational interest in software languages and engineering and technology. From the STEM programs, there's no doubt we'll see an amazing new group of software and hardware engineers.

Problems Appearing

We'll need all the brains we can bring to bear as we look to solve the problems of today and the problems of the future. After all, imagine a problem needs to be solved. This doesn't take much imagination, since there are innumerable problems in the world that need solutions. If you took paper and pencil and started writing them down, you could, theoretically, write forever.

Then, imagine a woman with four grown children goes back to college. She found, in raising her children, that she has a knack for putting things together. She spent hours and hours, on the carpet, building abstract shapes and tall buildings out of Legos, with them. But when she was growing up, she wasn't given boxes of Legos, Tinker Toys, or Lincoln Logs. This knack for building things is a revelation to her, and brings insights about her own talents and skills. She decides to go back to college, and switches her unfinished degree from English (and *nothing* wrong with an English degree) to computer science or engineering. She graduates, a few years later, with a degree in computer science or engineering. She even graduates at the top of her class.

At LinkResearchTools, we'd hire her in two seconds. We want to hire the best employees, because no matter how many software libraries serve up snippets of prewritten code to be stored and reused, no matter how many computer programs are written that tell computers how to write code, it is human beings, who will perceive what help humans need most. This is a reflection, of the fact, that humans are cooperative by nature and nurture. As adversarial, as we can be at times, cooperation brings the most rewards. Living on an island by yourself is pretty lonely. Just ask Robinson Crusoe. Everyone needs company.

Software Engineers Love Company

Software engineers are, regardless of reputation, convivial creatures. Being a software professional doesn't make us social hermits. It almost has the opposite effect. After all those hours spent at the computer, we get a bit...call it...*screen crazy* and need human contact. Honest.

Tony Hsieh, the founder of Zappos along with Nick Swinmurn, which was bought by Amazon for 1.2 Billion US dollars, had a bet with friends that if he was a millionaire, within ten years of college graduation, he'd pay for a cruise for all his friends. By early 1999, he and fifteen of his friends took that ocean cruise. The success of his online business made the cruise financially possible.

Hsieh writes, in his book, *Delivering Happiness: A Path To Profits, Passion, and Purpose,* that on the cruise, he and his friends "had a great time drinking, eating, partying, and then drinking, eating, and partying some more. It was like a mini college reunion."

Hsieh extended this love of companionship, as his financial ability grew. He bought real estate, what he came to call the "party loft," and for his twenty-sixth birthday had fog machines and lasers and disco balls and black lights decorating the loft. Tony had more than one-hundred people celebrating his birthday party with him. Later that year, celebrating New Year's Eve, the over-active fog machine brought the firemen and the fire trucks to "join" the party; the fog machines had set off the fire alarms.

Later, after an economic crunch, Hsieh sold the party loft.

Artificial Intelligence Is Coming

One of the big worries being bandied about in the software industry is the *increasing* intelligence of artificial intelligence. Hopefully our fellow humans will put the brakes on artificial intelligence if AI starts thinking it's in charge...of us.

We will always, if we maintain a premise of self-preservation, retain control of the code. Sure, we can use AI for crunching massive amounts of data, as Nate Silver is known to do with political or baseball data, or to assist us in writing a software program that teaches an autistic kid better interpersonal communication, or creates an accurate algorithm to bounce radar or lasers off the earth, so we establish exactly where the boundaries of countries are and avoid future conflict. The responsibility to maintain constraints, to limit artificial intelligence and keep it corralled, is ours. We can never let artificial intelligence "forget," *who is in charge*.

In his essay, at the SXSW Conference in 2009, Mark Zuckerberg cited the famous and ubiquitous coder maxim:

Code Wins Arguments

What he meant is when something works, functions, and creates value and the desired result, it's good. When it doesn't work, doesn't function, and doesn't create value or the desired result, it's not good. The desired result, in this case, is continued human control. In other words, we have to write the code that retains *human dominance*. Artificial intelligence can't possibly know what is best for humans, and we must remember that exigent point.

So Close, The Future

The role of software engineers will become more influential, not to just write software programs. We need software engineers to debate, with us, the significant questions of the future. Their very closeness, to the belly of the beast, ensures insight no one else can have.

Smart People Thinking About AI

So, are humans headed towards a future where we are living in a world, conceived by, our AI masters? Consigned to living as the slaves of our AI masters, shining their pretty, metal robot bodies and oiling their metal joints?

Elon Musk brings this question up when he's interviewed or speaks at a conference, frequently and with intensity. He's concerned that the answer doesn't favor humans being in control. In my estimation, if Elon Musk is concerned, the rest of us should be concerned.

Bill Gates pondered the evolution of computers into truly powerful machines, in 1995, as one of the points he made in *The Road Ahead*:

Others, hope or fear it will create computers as smart as human beings.

Elon Musk doesn't hope that computers will be as smart as human beings. Rather, he perceives computers, as an existential threat to human life, because they will be *so much smarter* than human beings. He says, "Artificial intelligence will beat humans at everything within the next few decades." He refers to AI, as "humanity's biggest risk."

To create the future we want, the one where we are in charge and not AI, we can take two steps that will support human input and control and continue our preeminence.

The Software Two-Step

First, we can recognize *International Programmer's Day* with all the flair it deserves, unlike its current state of "*International Programmer's Day*? What's that? You mean those weird guys and their weird computer languages?"

I mentioned *International Programmer's Day*, in the introduction and so I hesitate to mention it again, but maybe I have personal prejudices on this topic. I've seen, and been, a programmer pushing through code, trying to make it work, writing so late into the night that it's turned into morning. But even for those of us, who love our jobs, there's no doubt it's exhausting to write code. Neuron burning. But does anyone care…
˙ck no.

The other day I heard, almost endlessly, about it being "pickle day." Pickle day! Sure, pickles are great, but how much do they add to our lives? More conversation and celebration for *International Programmer's Day*, please.

Berkeley Breathed is one of the great thinkers of our time, a philosopher and sage. Some don't realize that he *disguises* himself as a cartoonist, albeit a cartoonist, who won the Pulitzer Prize for Editorial Cartooning, in 1987. As with Breathed's book, *Mars Needs Moms* (Take out the trash. Eat your broccoli. Who needs moms, anyway?), which pays significant homage to the importance of moms, there are could be better presentations in the media of software engineers. Maybe Breathed will write a sequel and title it: *Mars Needs Software Engineers*.

The book would give software engineers credit, for all this neat stuff, we use every day; show them a bit of appreciation, for their long hours over hot computers. This is way overdue.

Second, you can share this book with friends, family, cohorts, and spouses, and anyone else, who still thinks that software engineers live on pizza, shun daylight, and are socially inept. Their representation need not be black-hat, bat-pooh crazy all the time, as the software engineers seen in *Silicon Valley* and *Halt and Catch Fire* are portrayed. We could have a *Leave-It-To-Beaver* software engineer dad, or a Hans Solo, handsome-as-Harrison-Ford, software engineer dad, in a tv show or a movie.

And by the way, at LinkResearchTools:

We hire wookies who can code

We hire cookies who can code

We hire tall and short, thin and plump

We hire those who overcome coding humps.

So if you'd like to live in beautiful Austria, send emails with a "Hello World from Sunny Vienna!" greeting, drink a glass of wine while boating along the Danube, visit dozens of magnificent castles (sure, the United States – for instance – is a bigger country, *but it has no castles*!), hear some of the best opera in the world (The Bregenz Festival operas held at Lake Constance, as movie buffs know, was the backdrop location for the Bond movie, *Quantum of Solace*), and nibble our famous pastries, in beautiful Austrian coffeehouses, send along a resume!

Just mail it to jobs@spaghetticodebook.com

PS And don't forget the alpine skiing! Or going to visit the penguins at Zoo Vienna!

Acknowledgements

I would like to thank my wife and kids for always reminding me about life, love and the world outside of my business world. I wouldn't be where I am without you.

Also, I want to thank my team at LinkResearchTools (LRT) for letting me and us grow beyond all limits expected. It's hard to see success in the long run if you are buried in everyday routine. This book and future books I work on help me reflect and give back so many learnings.

The amount of new learnings every day are countless and never stop.

Per my core values - Learn fast and develop yourself!

http://www.spaghetticodebook.com/corevalues

References

Introduction

1. http://www.spaghetticodebook.com/myspacewhatwentwrongseanpercivalspotify
2. http://www.spaghetticodebook.com/whatwasitliketoprogramtheommodore64
3. Fried, Jason, and Heinemeier Hansson, Jason, Rework (New York: Crown, 2010). ISBN: 978-0307463746
4. http://www.spaghetticodebook.com/amazonwebservicescloudoutageinternetcrashes
5. http://www.spaghetticodebook.com/alphabetgoogleevil

Chapter 1   Bits, Bytes, and Bugs

1. http://www.spaghetticodebook.com/amazondashbutton
2. http://www.spaghetticodebook.com/appleitunesfreeapps
3. Yourdon, Edward, *Nations At Risk: The Impact Of The Computer Revolution* (Yourdon, 1990) ISBN: 978-0136121282
4. Gates, Bill, *The Road Ahead* (New York: Viking, 1995) ISBN: 978-0453009218
5. http://www.spaghetticodebook.com/zoovienna
6. http://www.spaghetticodebook.com/britannicacomtechnology2bug
7. http://www.spaghetticodebook.com/year2000problem
8. *Space Cowboys*, 2000, Malpaso Productions
9. http://www.spaghetticodebook.com/universetoday
10. Walsh Burke, Anna Mae, The Plain Brown Wrapper Book Of Computers (New York, Putnam Publishing, 1982) ISBN: 978-0936602592

11. http://www.spaghetticodebook.com/44billionpeoplestilldonthaveinternet
12. http://www.spaghetticodebook.com/hourofcode
13. http://www.spaghetticodebook.com/loopsandbloops

Chapter 2   Moore's Law

1. Isaacson, Walter, *The Innovators: How A Group Of Geniuses, Hackers, And Geeks Created The Digital Revolution* (New York, Simon & Schuster, 2015) ISBN: 978-1476708706
2. http://www.spaghetticodebook.com/djkhaled
3. *The Big Short*, 2015, Plan B Entertainment
4. Krug, Steve, *Don't Make Me Think, Revisited: A Common Sense Approach to Web Usability* (San Francisco: Peachpit/New Riders, 2014) ISBN: 978-0321965516
5. Chua, Amy, Battle Hymn of the Tiger Mother (New York, Penguin Press, 2011) ISBN: 978-1594202841
6. http://www.spaghetticodebook.com/healthytippingpoint

Chapter 3   Version Control

1. De Marco, Tom and Lister, Timothy, *Dancing With Bears: Managing Risk On Software Projects* (New York, Dorset House, 2003) ISBN: 978-09932633606
2. http://www.spaghetticodebook.com/google2billionlinescode
3. http://www.spaghetticodebook.com/sizeofgooglesourcecodelines
4. http://www.spaghetticodebook.com/grantcardone

Chapter 4   10X Better Is Just A Start

1. Isaacson, Walter, *Steve Jobs* (New York: Simon & Schuster, 2011) ISBN: 978-1451648539
2. Byrne, Rhonda, *The Secret* (New York: Atria Books/Beyond Words, 2006) ISBN: 978-1582701707
3. *Malice*, 1993, Castle Rock Entertainment

References

Chapter 5   Death Marching

1. Ries, Eric, *The Lean Startup: How Today's Entrepreneurs Use Continuous Innovation To Create Radically Successful Businesses* (New York: Currency, 2011) ISBN: 978-0307887894
2. http://www.spaghetticodebook.com/towritesoftwarereadnovels
3. Yourdon, Edward, *Rise & Resurrection of the American Programmer* (Yourdon Press Computing Series, 1996) ISBN: 978-0131218314
4. *Swordfish*, 2001, Village Roadshow Pictures
5. Maslow, Abraham, "A Theory of Human Motivation" *Psychological Review*, 1943.

Chapter 6   Feature Creep

1. http://www.spaghetticodebook.com/redditalexa
2. *Her*, 2013, Annapurna Pictures
3. http://www.spaghetticodebook.com/amazonsechodotisgreatbut
4. http://www.spaghetticodebook.com/appleiphone6svsiphone8xupgrade2017

Chapter 7   Onboarding

1. *I, Robot*, 2004, Overbrook Films
2. http://www.spaghetticodebook.com/siliconvalleycompanies-suedoveragreementsnottohire
3. http://www.spaghetticodebook.com/how70interestusersweddingthemedboards

Chapter 8   Minimum Viable Product

1. http://www.spaghetticodebook.com/cokelorenewcoke
2. Horowitz, Ben, *The Hard Thing About Hard Things: Building a Business When There Are No Easy Answers* (New York: HarperBusiness, 2014) ISBN: 978-0062273208

3. Hsieh, Tony, *Delivering Happiness: A Path to Profits, Passion, and Purpose* (New York: Grand Central Publishing, 2010) ISBN: 978-0446563048

Chapter 9   Freemium

1. Smith, Adam, The Wealth of Nations (England: William Strahan, 1776)
2. http://www.spaghetticodebook.com/oceanwildthings
3. http://www.spaghetticodebook.com/netflixraisingpriceitsmostpopularplan
4. http://www.spaghetticodebook.com/youtubeintroducesyoutubered

Chapter 10   Hotfix

1. http://www.spaghetticodebook.com/computerhope
2. *MacGyver*, Henry Winkler/John Rich Productions, 1985-1992
3. http://www.spaghetticodebook.com/featurecreep

Chapter 11   Waterfall Optimism

1. Cardone, Grant, *The 10X Rule: The Only Difference Between Success and Failure* (New York, Wiley, 2011) ISBN: 978-0470627600
2. Thiel, Peter, *Zero To One:* Notes on Startups, or How to Build the Future (New York: Crown, 2014) ISBN: 978-0804139298
3. Cardone, Grant, *If You're Not First, You're Last: Sales Strategies to Dominate Your Market and Beat Your Competition* (New York: Wiley, 2010)
4. http://www.spaghetticodebook.com/howcomplainingrewiresyourbrainnegativity

Chapter 12   24/7

1. Benioff, Marc, *Behind the Cloud: The Untold Story of How Salesforce.com Went from Idea to Billion-Dollar Company-and Revolutionized an Industry* (New Jersey: Jossey-Bass, 2009) ISBN: 978-0470521168

2. http://www.spaghetticodebook.com/seoktoberfest

Chapter 13 Garbage In, Garbage Out

1. *WarGames*, 1983, Sherwood Productions
2. http://www.spaghetticodebook.com/elonmuskhyperloop
3. http://www.spaghetticodebook.com/theonion

Chapter 14 Can You Quickly

1. Gawande, Atul, *The Checklist Manifesto: How To Get Things Right* (New York: Metropolitan Books, 2009) ISBN: 978-0805091748
2. http://www.spaghetticodebook.com/howwaspenicillindiscovered

Chapter 15 Batch Process

1. Ferriss, Tim, The 4-Hour Workweek (New York: Random/Harmony, 2009) ISBN: 978-0307465351
2. Csikszentmihalyi, Michael, *Finding Flow: The Psychology of Optimal Experience* (New York: Basic Books, 1997) ISBN: 978-0465024117
3. http://www.spaghetticodebook.com/headsmashedin
4. http://www.spaghetticodebook.com/realcostofnotpayingattention
5. http://www.spaghetticodebook.com/reddit

Chapter 16 Big Data

1. http://www.spaghetticodebook.com/searchengineland
2. http://www.spaghetticodebook.com/googlemaybeatmercyoffoesineuropeanantitrustbattle
3. O'Neil, Cathy, *Weapons of Math Destruction: How Big Data Increases Inequality and Threatens Democracy* (New York: Crown, 2016) ISBN: 978-0553418811
4. *The Big Short: Inside The Doomsday Machine,* 2015, Plan B Entertainment
5. http://www.spaghetticodebook.com/microsoftsupdatedprivacypolicy

Chapter 17 Wookies, Coders, & Our AI Masters

1. http://www.spaghetticodebook.com/python
2. http://www.spaghetticodebook.com/sxsw
3. http://www.spaghetticodebook.com/markzuckerberg
4. Breathed, Berkeley, *Mars Needs Moms* (New York: Scholastic, 2012) ISBN: 978-0545251808

Index

10X developers 59
Abraham Maslow 84
abstraction muscle 74, 80, 81
abstraction skill 75
Adam Smith 114
advertisement selling company 185
Alec Baldwin 67
Alexa 85, 87, 182
Alexander Fleming 162
Alexandria 51, 52
algorithm 27, 183, 192, 202
Altair 141, 142
Amazon 7, 10, 16, 67, 85, 87, 88, 108, 109, 173, 182, 201
Amy Chua 43
anachronistic dilemmas 9
antitrust activities? 188
Antonio Villas-Boas 89
Apple 31, 49, 64, 68
Arthur C. Clarke 121
artificial intelligence 21, 202, 203
Artificial intelligence 204
Atari 199

avoidable failures 163
backlink 6
backlinks 5, 28
Backlinks 5
BAFTA 36
BASIC 21
Battle Hymn of the Tiger Mother 43
Behind the Cloud 140
Ben Horowitz 103, 108, 136, 157
Beowulf 27
Berkeley Breathed 205
Bertha von Suttner 147
Best Buy 15
BGR 54
biblical principle 65
big data 190
Bill Gates 19, 20, 21, 114, 140, 156, 199, 204
Bill Murray 166
bits and bytes 13
black-hat 10, 11, 27
Bolshevik revolution 139
Brad Pitt 191

214

Bregenz Festival 206

bunny rabbit 181

Business Insider 89

California Employment Law Report 97

Captain Hook 158

carpal tunnel 124

Cathy O'Neil 190

CBS News Report, 7

CERN 30

chocolate eggs 181

Christoph Waltz 70

Clint Eastwood 28

Coco Chanel 83

Coke 102

college humanities 76

Commodore 15

Commodore 64 14, 164

communications satellites 29

computer game 11

computer illiterate 197

Consumer Supported Agriculture 152

Corning 66

creative process 75

dance of litigation 189

Dash buttons 16

David Heinemeier Hansson 8, 131

death march 9, 71

Delivering Happiness\ A Path To Profits, Passion, and Purpose 202

DJ Khaled 35

Donald Sutherland 28

Don't Be Evil 10

Don't Make Me Think 41

Do The Right Thing 10

Dr. Atul Gawande 160

Edward Yourdon 19, 77

Einstein 148

Elon Musk 203

ergonomic problems 124

Eric Ries 71

Erwin Schrödinger 49

Etsy 102

European Union 188

existential threat 204

Facebook 6, 10, 123, 173

Falco 111

feature creep 84

Finding Flow 173

first language 61

forcing functions 163

Franz Kafka 130

Freemium 118

Index

Genghis Khan 7
George S. Patton 59
Godzilla 27
Google 54
Gordon Moore 35
Grant Cardone 57, 131, 132, 134, 137, 165
Grendel 27
Groundhog Day 166
Habsburg 22
Harrison-Ford 205
Hello World 14, 206
Her 86
Hewlett Packard 20
Hollywood 32
hotfixing 127
Hugh Jackman 79
Hummer 36
If You're Not First, You're Last 137
IMDB 148
Ingeborg Bachmann 168
Intel 35, 38
International Programmer's Day 32, 83, 204
internet neighborhood 6
internet of things 15
iOS 16, 31
I, Robot 95

Isaacson 39, 77
James Garner 28
Jason Fried 8, 131
JavaScript 33
J. Bradford Hipps 76
Jeff Bezos 67, 175
Jerry Seinfeld 181
Joaquin Phoenix 86
John Lasseter 66
Jon Ive 66
Khan Academy 32
Laurene Powell 64
Leave It To Beaver 205
Legos 201
LinkedIn 123
link farms 5, 6
LinkResearchTools 6, 40, 68, 74, 114, 164, 201, 205
MacGyver 122
Madame Curie 147
magic box 17
Malice 67
Marc Andreessen 103
Marc Benioff 140
Marc Zuckerberg 203
Mark Zuckerberg 199, 203
Mars Needs Moms 205

Matthew 21\
22 65
Matthew Broderick 148
Michael Burry 191
Michael Corleone 34
Microsoft 10, 20, 141, 156, 187
Microsoft Office 185
Mihaly Csikszentmihalyi 172
Moore's Law 34, 37, 38, 39, 44, 209
Mother Teresa 188
Motley Fool 88
Myspace 123
NASA 28
Nate Silver 202
National Geographic 18
Nations At Risk 19
Netflix 113, 119
Netflix, 119
Nick Swinmurn 201
Nicole Kidman 67
Niki Lauda 13
NINJA loans 36
Nobel Prize 147
Norman Vincent Peale 65
Ocean Wild Things 115
odd snippets 18
Oskar Kokoschka 92

Paul Allen 20, 141
Pavlov's dogs 157
Paypal 199
Peacetime CEO 158
Penguin 23, 26, 27, 28
Penguin, 5
penicillin 162
Pepsi 102
Peter Pan 158
Peter Thiel 135
philosophers 161
Pierre Omidyar 199
Pinterest 94, 95
Pizza 19
Popular Electronics 141, 142, 143
potlatch 36
public opinion 10
Pulitzer Prize 205
Python 196
quantum computing 13, 38, 39
qubit 38
Rachel Potvin 53
Reddit 85, 180
Rework 8, 131
Rhonda Byrne 65
Robert Noyce 39
Robinson Crusoe 201

Index

Rupert Murdoch 178
Samsung 35
Schönbrunn Palace 22
Sean Percival 4
SearchEngineLand 182
Self-fulfilling prophecies 40
self-motivation ethic 175
SEOktoberfest 145
September 13th 32
Serapeum 52
Sigmund Freud 56
slice of software 8
smart home 17
smartphone 16
smartphones 30
software apps 16
software engineers 10, 54, 74
Software Engineers 18
software program 6
software programmers 10, 40
Software programmers 60
software programs 18, 196
Space Cowboys 28, 29
spaghetti code 9, 23, 31
Stanley Kubrick 121
STEM programs 200
Stephen King 22

Steve Jobs 19, 20, 62, 63, 64, 65, 66, 76, 209
Steve Krug 41
Steve Wozniak 62, 66
Stoics 17
Swordfish 79
SXSW Conference 203
TechCrunch 87
Tech Target 153
Tesla 126
The 4-Hour Workweek 168, 169, 170, 179
The 10X Rule 132
The Big Short 36, 191
The Checklist Manifesto 160
The Godfather 34
The Hard Thing about Hard Things 136
The Hard Thing About Hard Things 103, 157
the human race 199
The Innovators 34, 39
the law of attraction 47
The Lean Startup 71
The Matrix 17
The New York Times 75
Theodore Roosevelt 101
The Onion 152

The Penguin 5, 26

The Plain Brown Wrapper Book Of Computers 30

The Road Ahead 21, 140, 204, 208

The Second Great Scare 23

The Secret 65

The Wealth of Nations 114

Tim Berners-Lee 30

Tim Ferriss 168, 175, 177, 179

Tim Lister 53

Timothy Lister 103

Tom DeMarco 53, 103

Tommy Lee Jones 28

Tony Hsieh 107, 201

tracking packet 197

Travis Bradberry 137

Twitter 173

UniverseToday 29

Van Gogh 84

venture capital 158

version control 50

Version control 55

Vienna Zoo 22, 23

vision 63

vitamin P 19, 194

Walsh Burke 30

Walter Isaacson 34

Waltzing with Bears 103

Waltzing With Bears 53

WarGames 148

Warren Buffett 178

Wartime CEO 158

waterfall process 130

Weapons of Math Destruction 190

weight loss advice 6

Western mothers 43

white-hat 11

Wiener Schnitzel 45

Wikipedia 199

William Shakespeare 139

Will Smith 95

Windows 16, 31

Wired 173

Wolfgang Puck 196

World Heritage Sites 176

Y2k 23, 31

YouTube 35, 113, 182

YouTube Red 113

Zappos 107, 108, 109, 157, 201

Zero To One 135

Zoo Vienna 206

Resources

The LinkResearchTools Academy – Training Material, eBooks and Videos for Online Marketers

http://www.spaghetticodebook.com/academy

Christoph C. Cemper's personal website

http://www.spaghetticodebook.com/christoph

Christoph C. Cemper's YouTube Channel

http://www.spaghetticodebook.com/youtube

Christoph C. Cemper's Instagram Profile

http://www.spaghetticodebook.com/instagram

Christoph C. Cemper's LinkedIn Profile

http://www.spaghetticodebook.com/linkedin

Christoph C. Cemper's Twitter Account

http://www.spaghetticodebook.com/twitter

Christoph C. Cemper's Amazon Author Profile

http://www.spaghetticodebook.com/amazon

LinkResearchTools (LRT) – core values

http://www.spaghetticodebook.com/corevalues

LinkResearchTools (LRT) – the software product

http://www.spaghetticodebook.com/lrtcom (website in English)

http://www.spaghetticodebook.com/lrtde (website in German)

Author Biography

"SEO is an experimental science, do not blindly follow the old rules."
CHRISTOPH C. CEMPER

Christoph C. Cemper began working with online marketing in 2003, providing search engine organization (SEO) consulting and link-building services to businesses and business professionals. Due to a pressing need for reliable, comprehensive, and accurate SEO software, he developed an internal tool for his own business, in 2006, that could verify links associated with websites.

This initial software *tool* became a baseline product, and evolved into the company's complete software service, LinkResearchTools (LRT). This software suite launched to the public in 2009, a SaaS product with four tools.

The goal of the company, and its software suite, was to ensure that each business controlled their *link associations* on the internet. By doing so, the business controlled their image and brand name; the LRT software allowed them to disavow links to websites, which they felt were discordant with their values and image.

The importance of a business recovering from Google penalties, protecting against future penalties, outgrowing their competitors, and increasing their traffic through proactive link building becomes imperative, as the search engines gain greater control and power.

When the famous Google Penguin update changed the rules of SEO in 2012, Christoph launched Link Detox®, a software built for finding links that posed a risk in a website's backlink profile, and introduced the technology and formal process for ongoing link audits in 2012, as well as pro-active removal and disavowal of *bad* links.

Christoph focuses on leading his team to remain cutting edge in staying informed, and adapting to, any changes to search engine algorithms that affect the company's clients and their businesses. In the post-Penguin era, every link-building mistake can lead to a Google penalty resulting in lost business.

Thanks to ongoing development and continuous testing, LinkResearchTools provides dozens of SEO tools, with ever-growing power, functionality adapted to market requirements, and the algorithmic changes from Google, Bing, Yahoo, and other search engine changes updated as needed.

In 2015, Christoph launched Impactana®, a unique "Content Marketing Intelligence" technology, which supports marketing professionals seeking content ideas that make an impact.

Christoph has been speaking and writing about *link risk management* and search engine organization, since early 2011. He is multilingual (German and English) and a renowned speaker, presenting at more than 300 high-profile search engine organization conferences. As well, LinkResearchTools sponsors a variety of charity events, including the SEOktoberfest, held in Munich each year and attended by top-level SEO experts, with proceeds provided to humanitarian organizations.

In Progress: Entrepreneurship Book

As an entrepreneur, Christoph C. Cemper is dedicated to sharing the failures and successes, from his many years in business, with others. These failures and successes taught him invaluable business lessons. And by sharing them, he hopes to support others, as they endeavor to create entrepreneurial businesses. As such, he is currently at work on his second book. The topic of the second book is entrepreneurship and achieving goals.

Printed in Poland
by Amazon Fulfillment
Poland Sp. z o.o., Wrocław